Posttraumatic Growth in Clinical Practice

From the authors who pioneered the concept of posttraumatic growth comes *Posttraumatic Growth in Clinical Practice*, a book that brings the study of growth after trauma into the twenty-first century. Clinicians will find a framework that is easy to use and flexible enough to be tailored to the needs of particular clients and specific therapeutic approaches. And, because it utilizes a model of relating described as "expert companionship," clinicians learn how to become most empathically effective in helping a variety of trauma survivors. Clinicians will come away from this book having learned how to assess posttraumatic growth, how to address it in treatment, and they will also have a basic grasp of the ways the changes they are promoting will be received in various cultural contexts. Case examples show how utilizing a process developed from an empirically-based model of posttraumatic growth can promote important personal changes in the aftermath of traumatic events.

Lawrence G. Calhoun, PhD, is Professor of Psychology at UNC Charlotte and a licensed psychologist. Together with Richard Tedeschi, he is one of the pioneers in the development of research and theory on posttraumatic growth. He teaches undergraduate and graduate students and is a recipient of the Bank of America Award for Teaching Excellence and of the University of North Carolina Board of Governors' Award for Teaching Excellence.

Richard G. Tedeschi, PhD, is Professor of Psychology at UNC Charlotte, where he teaches personality and psychotherapy. He is a licensed psychologist specializing in bereavement and trauma and has led support groups for bereaved parents since 1987. He serves as a consultant to the American Psychological Association on trauma and resilience.

Together, Tedeschi and Calhoun have published several books, including the *Handbook of Posttraumatic Growth: Research and Practice* (Routledge, 2006) and *Helping Bereaved Parents: A Clinician's Guide* (Routledge, 2004).

Posttraumatic Growth in Clinical Practice

LAWRENCE G. CALHOUN AND
RICHARD G. TEDESCHI

NEW YORK AND LONDON

First published 2013
by Routledge
711 Third Avenue, New York, NY 10017

Simultaneously published in the UK
by Routledge
27 Church Road, Hove, East Sussex BN3 2FA

Routledge is an imprint of the Taylor & Francis Group, an informa
business

The right of Lawrence G. Calhoun and Richard G. Tedeschi to be
identified as authors of this work has been asserted by them in
accordance with sections 77 and 78 of the Copyright, Designs and
Patents Act 1988.

Library of Congress Cataloging in Publication Data
Calhoun, Lawrence G.
Posttraumatic growth in clinical practice / Lawrence G. Calhoun and
Richard G. Tedeschi.
p. cm.
Includes bibliographical references and index.
1. Post-traumatic stress disorder--Treatment. 2. Post-traumatic stress
disorder--Patients--Rehabilitation. I. Tedeschi, Richard G. II. Title.
RC552.P67C45 2013
616.85'21--dc23
2012025059

ISBN: 978-0-415-89869-0 (hbk)
ISBN: 978-0-415-64530-0 (pbk)
ISBN: 978-0-203-62904-8 (ebk)

Typeset in Minion
by Fakenham Prepress Solutions, Fakenham, Norfolk NR21 8NN

To Mary Lynne, Eliza, and Mary Laura, amazing and beautiful women who have changed my life and who are changing the world.

LGC

To my sweet teachers about living life well—Curly Girl, and her friends Puppet Cow and Tiger. Thanks for our many conversations.

RGT

Contents

Preface

Clinicians who work with clients who have experienced major life stressors will, sooner or later, encounter clients who have experienced posttraumatic growth. Although there has been some preliminary work on interventions that include growth components, there is still much that is not known. This book draws on the current research on posttraumatic growth, but a main foundation is our combined experience as practicing clinicians. We have talked with many people who experienced positive change from their struggles with traumatic events and we have seen many clients whose encounter with tragedy has also produced changes that, for them, are valued highly.

This book presents what research has shown us about the phenomenon of growth that arises from the struggle with tragedy. It also represents what we have learned from all of those who have shared with us their suffering and their losses, and also those who have shared their sometimes extraordinary transformations. We have written a book designed to provide helpful suggestions to practicing clinicians, whose professional training is in a wide array of disciplines, including clinical and counseling psychology, counseling, clinical social work, pastoral counseling, and others. But we have also tried to make the book easily accessible to laypersons.

In the service of utility and reader-friendliness, our citation of references is illustrative rather than exhaustive. We have given specific examples and cited individual cases throughout this book. We have provided examples from actual therapy sessions, but have altered information to protect confidentiality and assure anonymity. In some chapters we provide an overview of the current state of the work in a particular area and provide some illustrative case material. In other chapters we focus primarily on what we actually say in sessions regarding posttraumatic growth, and we comment on how these interventions reflect good clinical practice generally, and how they reflect the sensitive practice of trauma therapy that we call *expert companionship*.

Acknowledgments

We have been very fortunate. We have worked for many years in an academic department that is collegial and supportive, and that encourages scholarly collaboration. We have found not only outstanding professional colleagues with whom to work, but those colleagues are also our good friends. We are grateful to have such a good colleague and distinguished psychologist as our Chair, Fary Cachelin.

Although he is not a co-author of this book, our great friend and gifted social psychologist Arnie Cann has contributed immeasurably to many of the ideas on which we rely. He has generously shared his expertise as we have worked together to better understand the general processes of coping with highly stressful events, and posttraumatic growth in particular.

She is relatively new to our department, but we consider ourselves very fortunate to have been given the opportunity to work with Amy Canevello, also a social psychologist, whose work shows great promise for broadening the understanding of posttraumatic growth in close relationships.

Our colleague and good friend, Charlie Reeve, has been an invaluable resource with the complexities of research design and statistical analysis.

For three extraordinary years we were joined by Dr. Kana Taku, currently on the faculty of Oakland University in Michigan. She has greatly expanded the borders of our understanding of responses to traumatic events.

We have also been granted the privilege of working with a gifted group of graduate students in recent years: Jessica Groleau, Elizabeth Addington, Cassie Lindstrom, Tanya Vishnevsky, Kelli Triplett, Michelle Jesse, Amanda D'Angelo, and Manolya Calisir.

Most of all, we wish to acknowledge the clients with whom we have worked and the many persons who faced great personal tragedies who generously shared their experiences with us. They have demonstrated to us the importance of staying open to the possibility that from great suffering can come great wisdom and growth. They have taught us that, as professionals with expertise, sometimes our best gift is to simply be a trusted companion for a long and difficult journey.

one
The Process of Posttraumatic Growth in Clinical Practice

He did not marry until he was 39, several months after he met the woman he described as being "my perfect match." She was three years older—successful, intelligent, warm, highly educated, with the same core values. They both wanted children, but knew that the chances of having their own biological children diminished with each year.

They were delighted when her pregnancy was confirmed in their third year of marriage. Their baby boy was born without incident, and he developed quickly and precociously. As the years passed, however, the parents slowly drifted apart. Her job required her to travel frequently and his required him to work long hours, often into late night. That combination proved fatal to what had been a thriving and happy relationship. When the boy was nine the marriage ended, but the divorce was civilized and amicable. They decided that the circumstances made it wiser for him to assume primary custody, with visitation whenever she would like. Things remained amicable and peaceful in the now separated family.

However, during the boy's first year of high school, things started to go wrong. His teachers reported that his performance in school was suffering. In spite of being very intelligent and capable, his grades became poor. On some days he had great difficulty getting ready for school, moving slowly and complaining that he did not want to go. On others, he was extremely irritable. The parents sought professional help.

The clinician indicated that the boy was clinically depressed and recommended psychotherapy and a medical consultation for antidepressants. Medication was prescribed and psychotherapy sessions began and continued for the next months. However, his depression did not abate. He was moody and angry, stayed in his room most of the time when he was not at school, he had no friends, and showed little interest in engaging in any activities beyond lying in his bed.

Neither his parents nor the professionals who had been seeing him expected it when it happened. One evening, when his father went to his room to call him to supper, he found him hanging from the back of the door. He had used his belt—it should not have worked, but it did. Although the emergency medical team went through the motions, it was clear that they could not revive him. At the age of 14, his first suicide attempt had been successful.

The father sought professional help and started regular sessions with an experienced, caring, and empathetic clinician. A clear element in his distress was his overwhelming sense of guilt at having "failed my son." From his perspective, he believed he should have been able not only to foresee, but also to prevent his son's suicidal death. Although the clinician would sometimes provide gentle reassurance and occasional gentle probing of the degree to which the sense of guilt was truly merited, the clinician's main contribution was simply to listen, using his expertise occasionally and then only when it appeared useful to the grieving father.

As time progressed and the father's distress was somewhat reduced, the clinician began to notice something intriguing in the clinical sessions. In the midst of describing his continuing sense of guilt, his sadness, and his continued yearning for his son, the father would sometimes talk about how his struggle and pain had changed him—being forced by suffering "to be a better man, a different man. I am not who I used to be. I am permanently wounded, a man who will never be whole again. But I am also stronger than I thought I would be, and I find my heart going out to other parents whose children suffer or other parents who have had to face the kind of hell I have been forced to live in. Maybe I can use my pain to somehow help others live through theirs."

How should clinicians respond to, and deal with, not only the great pain and suffering that this father had to endure, but also his reports of being a better person and wanting to help others, as a result of having to walk through his own personal valley of the shadow? Although some professionals specialize in working exclusively with survivors of traumatic events, or with persons dealing with grief and loss, even those who do not have such specialty practices will have clients like this father. Or they will see people who have been traumatized in other ways, or who have faced other major life crises and severe stressors. This book suggests a particular stance to take in working with persons facing these kinds of very difficult struggles. The perspective described here is not an alternative to be used instead of the demonstrably effective therapeutic approaches for helping people deal with the aftermath of traumatic events. What we describe in this book is a therapeutic perspective that adds to and expands best practices. This book is about posttraumatic growth in clinical practice and the therapeutic stance of the *expert companion* for working with persons facing major difficulties in life. However, before focusing on growth it is important to be reminded that life crises can bring significant distress.

The Negative Side of Life Crises

People who have personal experience with traumatic events[1] and clinicians who have worked with them know that, although many persons can be resilient or can bounce back quickly in the face of trauma, negative reactions are common and pervasive (Bonanno, 2004; Keane, Marshall, & Taft, 2006). More extensive description of the kinds of psychological distress persons facing major life crises can be found elsewhere, but it is important to be reminded that in spite of great resilience, human beings can also experience significant distress when they encounter trauma. The present description will provide only a brief summary of some of the most common reactions.

Distressing Emotions

A general rule of thumb is that the more prolonged the exposure and the more intensely negative the circumstances are, the more likely it is that people will experience distressing emotions. For persons exposed to life-threatening events a major emotional response is anxiety and fear, particularly about the future occurrence of similar events. A woman who seeks shelter from a physically abusive relationship, for example, may have great concern about her physical safety. In the aftermath of the devastating tornados that strike various parts of the United States every year, a common response is worry and apprehension when skies become dark, cloudy, and rainy.

The specific emotions will vary with the person and the circumstance, but most people, even highly resilient people, will experience some degree of distress in situations that are challenging. Sadness is recognized as an almost universal reaction to the death of a loved one. It is typical for bereaved persons to be sad, yearn for the deceased, and wish that things could have been different (Neimeyer, Harris, Winokuer, & Thornton, 2011).

As it was with the father described above, guilt is not uncommon among persons dealing with life crises. Guilt has elements of both thoughts and emotions, but the guilt that most clinicians will encounter in their clients is a *feeling of guilt*. Survivor guilt is a common response for persons who have survived a catastrophe that did not spare others. For example, the mother of a child who was recovering from a very serious school bus accident began to feel a great sense of guilt over her joy that her child had survived, when that same crash had killed several other children.

The sense of guilt may be tied to ruminations about what the person might have done, should have done, or should have left undone (Gilbar, Plivazky, & Gil, 2010). The 16-year-old daughter of a woman who was hospitalized for a brief and routine operation had a heated argument with her mother about the use of the family car and stormed out of her mother's room and left for the night—her mother died of unexpected complications only a few hours later. The daughter was troubled for a long time by the guilt she felt over that last encounter with her mother.

Anger and irritability are also common responses to major stressors. Although these are usually not regarded as having the same clinical significance as anxiety or depression, these are not pleasant emotions. The anger may be expressed directly at those believed to be responsible for the event, like the man whose job is lost to "downsizing" and who later returns well-armed thinking about killing those whom he believes cost him his job. But the irritation and anger may be focused on targets unrelated to the event. For example, a man whose mother was in hospice care became furious at the "total lack of care my mother is getting," although hospice was providing quite good care for his dying mother.

Unwelcome Intruders: Distressing Thoughts and Images

Re-experiencing the event is one of the symptoms of posttraumatic stress disorder. Most people who are exposed to traumatic events do not develop the disorder, but they may well experience repeated intrusions into consciousness of memories of traumatic events, sometimes in the form of images but more commonly in the form of intrusive thoughts. "I keep thinking about it, but I don't want to" describes a common response of persons facing difficult situations. A man recently diagnosed with prostate cancer, for example, found that even minor reminders would lead him to think, over and over again, about what would happen to him as he faced choices about treatments and the variety of possible outcomes that the illness and its treatment held for him.

The content of the intrusive thoughts will vary greatly, but intrusive thoughts are common and they will to be experienced as negative and unpleasant.

Problematic Behaviors and Physical Symptoms

Although not a typical response to major stressors, some people may begin or intensify problematic behaviors. One possibility is the problematic use of substances (Schwabe, Dickinson, & Wolf, 2011). The misuse of commonly available drugs, such as alcohol or tobacco, may be triggered or intensified by the occurrence of a major life crisis. For some people, the maladaptive or excessive use of food, as a way to provide some sense of psychological comfort, may also be a possibility.

The experience of distressing emotions is common, and some persons may assume that others cannot, or will not want to, listen, understand, or help in any significant way (Kaynak, Lepore, & Kliewer, 2011). People may then either withdraw from others, or fail to seek support in the ways that might be most useful, making support more difficult. If the person experiences significant depression or if the event involved elements of sexual violence, then another challenge may be the emergence of sexual difficulties.

Another behavioral problem may be an increase in the likelihood of aggressive behavior. A very cautious and tentative generalization is that anger and aggression may be somewhat more likely in men who are faced with significant life challenges. A particularly lethal combination is the excessive use of alcohol together with an increase in angry and aggressive behavior. People who are themselves survivors of childhood physical or sexual abuse may be at somewhat higher risk of engaging in similar behaviors as adults, and alcohol use can act as a disinhibitor for those undesirable behaviors.

The relationship between life stress and the presence of physical symptoms, and on occasion even physical illnesses, is widely recognized. Exposure to highly stressful events can place some people at risk for psychological problems, perhaps even posttraumatic stress disorder, and exposure to stressors can also increase the possibility of developing physical illnesses (Spitzer, Barnow, Volzke, Ulrich, Freyberger, & Grabe, 2009). Even if fully developed illnesses do not occur, people exposed to major life stressors may complain of a wide variety of physical discomforts.

The body's physical activation in response to stressful circumstances, what is described in general terms as the fight or flight response, can last for some time after a particular event is over. People will then report a variety of physical symptoms, probably depending on their genetic predispositions and previous health practices. Some possibilities are fatigue, gastrointestinal difficulties, a sense of being physically "nervous," trouble breathing, muscle tension and aches, difficulty sleeping, feeling jumpy, etc.

It is important for clinicians to recognize that some people dealing with the aftermath of a traumatic event can report such physical complaints. Under some circumstances a referral for medical evaluation may be necessary. But perhaps more often, the clinician needs simply to understand that this wide array of complaints represents the expected response of the body to the highly demanding situation the individual is facing.

Summary: The Negative Side

Highly challenging events can produce a wide range of unpleasant psychological and physical responses. The poet Ted Hughes described this possibility, in this way, when he referred to the impact of the suicidal deaths of his two wives, "I have an idea of these two episodes as giant steel doors shutting down over great parts of myself" (quoted in Allen 2002, p. 12). There are some exceptional people who will not experience even mild and temporary distress, but most people will likely go through a time where they feel psychologically or physically challenged. The type and pattern of the troubles will differ, but most people who face very difficult life circumstances are likely to experience distressing psychological states and perhaps some physical discomfort as well. In addition, individuals exposed to traumatic events may also be at risk for psychiatric disorders, such as PTSD (Posttraumatic Stress Disorder) and depression. It is important to keep in mind, however, that the emergence of psychiatric disorders appears to be the exception, rather than the rule.

The possibilities for distress emerging from the struggle with trauma have been recognized for many years by clinicians and by researchers. Practicing clinicians understandably have focused on the negative consequences of the struggle with crisis events, because their role is to help persons whose responses to trauma include distressing and painful responses for which they would like relief. But there has also been the recognition that life challenges can represent the paradoxical opportunity for the experience of growth in the very context that has produced discomfort, pain, and suffering.

Posttraumatic Growth: Background

Homer in *The Odyssey*, the story about Odysseus' long journey home from the Trojan War, says, "Even his griefs are a joy long after to one that remembers all that he wrought and endured." Paul, in the Christian New Testament, says "We also rejoice in our sufferings, because we know that suffering produces perseverance; and perseverance character." An African proverb tells us that "Smooth seas do not make skillful sailors."

As these quotations indicate, the idea that the encounter with major adversity can change some people for the better, perhaps in radical ways, is not new. Although we did introduce the term *posttraumatic growth* (Tedeschi & Calhoun, 1995) to label this experience, clearly we did not discover this phenomenon. The ideas and writings of the ancient Greeks, Hebrews, early Christians, the teachings of Buddhism, Hinduism, and Islam, all have addressed the possibility of good coming from suffering. In more recent times, thoughtful scholars like Frankl (1963), Caplan (1964), Dohrenwend (1978), and Yalom (1980) addressed the possibilities for positive change offered by the encounter with critical life problems.

We defined *posttraumatic growth* as the experience of positive change that the individual experiences as a result of the struggle with a traumatic event (Calhoun & Tedeschi, 1999). The systematic study of this phenomenon was energized in the mid-1990s by several factors. One was the publication of articles (O'Leary & Ickovics, 1995), and at least one book (Tedeschi & Calhoun, 1995), that called attention to the possibility that positive change could be set in motion by the encounter with difficult life situations. Another factor was the publication of inventories developed to measure self-reports of growth including the Changes in Outlook Questionnaire (Joseph, Williams, & Yule 1993), the Stress-Related Growth Scale (Park, Cohen, & Murch, 1996) and the Posttraumatic Growth Inventory (Tedeschi & Calhoun, 1996). A third contributing factor may have been the renewed call to focus more on the understanding of positive elements of human behavior, what has become the influential "positive psychology" movement (Seligman & Csikszentmihalyi, 2000).

The study of posttraumatic growth is now widespread, with investigations having been conducted in many countries, including the United States, Great Britain, Brazil, Australia, Chile, China, Germany, Malaysia, the Netherlands,

Portugal, Pakistan, India, Spain, Norway, Sweden, Denmark, and Japan. Entering the restricted term *posttraumatic growth* into the search engine Google produces more than 100,000 "hits." Entering the same phrase into *PsychInfo* results in over 650 references. In the remainder of this chapter, we will provide an overview of some of the findings about posttraumatic growth. We will first provide a description of the general ways in which posttraumatic growth is typically experienced. Following that, we will address the validity of reports of growth. Next we describe a general model of the process of growth, and the chapter will conclude with a discussion of the possibility of posttraumatic growth in couples, families, and communities.

The Experience of Posttraumatic Growth

When US Airways flight 1549 struck a flight of geese, lost all power to its engines, and was landed safely by its crew on the Hudson River in New York 15 January 2009, it was called "The Miracle on the Hudson." All on board were safely rescued. Recalling the impact of that experience, Pam Seagle, an executive with Bank of America said "I thought about my family, my family, my family." Since then she has shifted priorities to place more emphasis on her parents, husband, and her children. "I say 'I love you' to people I never said that to before" (Washburn, June 12, 2011).

No general summary can encompass every single element that all persons will report as part of their growth experience, but there does seem to be a set of general elements that are quite common. Statistically, the experience tends to be reflected in five factors (Brunet, McDonough, Hadd, Crocker, & Sabiston, 2010; Taku, Cann, Calhoun & Tedeschi, 2008; Tedeschi & Calhoun, 1996): personal strength, relating to others, new possibilities in life, appreciation of life, and spirituality. These five factors fall into three conceptual categories, as follows: a changed sense of oneself; a changed sense of relationships with others; and a changed philosophy of life.

Changed Sense of Self

"I am not who I was." Confrontation with suffering and difficulty changes people. One way in which change can happen is by making people unambiguously aware that life holds the potential for the unexpected and uncontrollable (Janoff-Bulman, 1992, 2006). This awareness can make people fearful and anxious, particularly when confronted with situations that are similar to the traumatic event. The occurrence of such bad things can also, paradoxically, lead some people to experience a positive change in the way they see themselves. A common way this positive change is described is with phrases like "I am much stronger than I ever imagined. If I am living through this I can live through just about anything" and "I had to deal with major suffering and little things don't get to me anymore."

This paradox of growth can be summarized with the phrase *more vulnerable, yet stronger.* Loss and suffering teach people, particularly those of us in the Western tradition of individualism, of belief in personal control, and of self-reliance, that bad things can happen to us, sometimes with no warning and in ways that permit us no control over the outcomes. Life crises remind us that difficult challenges are an inevitable part of life. But in the confrontation with major crises, some persons also come to the realization that they have abilities to cope and survive, and perhaps even prevail, that they did not realize they had. As Albert Camus once said, "In the midst of winter, I finally learned that there was in me an invincible summer."

One of the people we have talked to was a young man who had been severely injured when his all-terrain vehicle overturned. He had been driving the vehicle unsafely up a steep incline, he was not wearing a seat belt, and the vehicle had no protective roll bar. As he put it—"amazingly stupid."

He described the accident as having taught him just how strong he could be. He said that if he could handle the aftermath of a serious accident that hospitalized him for several weeks and forced him into months of physical and occupational therapy, he could handle just about anything that life could throw at him in the future. Having to deal with the consequences of the accident, in ways that to him were quite successful, had taught him that he had more resilience and strength than he could ever have imagined.

One of the widows we interviewed, in the very early years of our work on posttraumatic growth (before the term existed), was a woman in her early eighties whose husband had died about 18 months before. She lived alone in the same house that had been her home for the past 55 years. She was talking in the sun room of her house, that looked out on a rather large back yard. "There used to be a wire fence back there that I really hated. But Lloyd kind of liked it, because he grew peas on it. About six months after he died I was sitting here and looked at the fence and thought: Lloyd wouldn't mind if I took it down now." So, this elderly but quite feisty woman marched out to her backyard, by herself, and took down the wire fence. She rolled up the wire and dragged it to the curb for the trash-collection crew to pick up.

"I know bad stuff can happen to me, but I think I am much more capable of handling it than I was before I faced this" is the theme for many persons. But, the increased experience of general self-competence is strongly tempered by the sobering knowledge that "bad things can happen, bad things did happen, and they happened to me."

Changed Relationships

"You find out who your real friends are." Life crises test the quality of relationships and can certainly strain them. Parents who lose a child, for example, may find that the pain of loss, and perhaps different patterns of coping with the loss, may sometimes cause some dysfunction in their relationship (Rogers, Floyd, Seltzer,

Greenberg, & Hong, 2008). But dealing with a life crisis can also offer the possibility for a deepening and strengthening of relationships. A woman in her sixties, who had lost her husband to cancer a few months earlier, said: "I don't think I have ever been as close to my children as I have in the months since Harold died. I've gotten to know them in a way that somehow just didn't seem possible before. I think I'm more real and so are they, if that makes any sense." Another person said. "Although we had a pretty good marriage before, I think this forced us to look at what we meant to each other ... We vowed to make ourselves a better couple ... it reminds us each day we are going to be good partners."

A senior executive was diagnosed with a rare and serious form of cancer. His treatment required periodic leaves from work, so his condition became well-known to his co-workers. As the cycle of treatment, home for recovery, and return to work continued, he found himself focusing on what he called "the deeper stuff." When colleagues at work greeted him with a routine "how are you doing" he found himself wanting to avoid inconsequential social pleasantries and, at least with colleagues who seemed really interested, he began to speak honestly about things. He began to tell them a bit more about his treatment, what it was like, talking more with them about some of the "the deeper stuff." As one of those colleagues indicated, there was a reciprocal increase in meaningful responses from others, who then began to tell the executive about their own "deeper stuff"— particularly about their concern and care for him in his battle with cancer. Some of those relationships deepened and became important human connections both for the man with cancer and for some of his now close friends at work.

This greater freedom to express oneself is not uncommon. A widow we interviewed some years ago said, "I feel much freer to express my emotions now, because I went through a time when I couldn't hold them back anyway. And now I like it that I can let them just flow with people I trust." There can be a greater sense of freedom to talk about one's thoughts and feelings, but also a greater sense of allowing oneself to let others *see* the feelings and emotions. The encounter with suffering can lead people to be more honest, at least with trusted others, about how they feel and think, and to experience greater ease in expressing themselves emotionally to others.

Along with a sense of increased closeness and depth of relationships with specific people, those who have faced suffering may also experience an increased compassion for other human beings, especially those who suffer (Bauwens & Tosone, 2010). Parents who have lost a child, for example, can become much more aware of, and feel an empathic compassion for, other parents who experience a similar loss. Bereaved parents report feeling a greater sense of compassion for other parents affected by a similar painful loss, perhaps engaging in specific small acts of kindness, such as sending sympathy cards or attending funeral services (Tedeschi & Calhoun, 2004). Sometimes the increased sense of compassion can result in a stronger commitment to easing the suffering of others. A mother whose child died after a long battle with cancer decided to return to school to study nursing. She became an oncology nurse, specializing in pediatric cancer because she wanted to do what she could to make the lives of very sick children better, but perhaps more importantly for her, she wanted to provide assistance to parents whose children had to face difficult medical procedures.

Changed Philosophy of Life

Perhaps one of the most common growth experiences triggered by a major stressor is an increased appreciation of life. This may be particularly the case with situations that involve strong reminders of mortality—a diagnosis of cancer, an emergency landing in the Hudson river, or surviving a brief but terrifying armed robbery. The person may experience increased satisfaction in playing with a toddler, being more deeply touched by a beautiful sunset, or simply relishing the delight of spending time with warm and close friends. American veterans who experienced the brutal conditions in POW camps, for example, may report how they still relish the simple pleasures of eating a hot dog or licking an ice cream cone (Rodman, Engdahl, Tedeschi, & Calhoun, 2002). An encounter with a traumatic event can provide the strong lesson that much of what we love is temporary, so we should deliberately engage with the important parts of our lives while we can.

In his memoir of his battle with three types of cancer, Hamilton Jordan (2000, p. 216), Chief of Staff of the White House for President Jimmy Carter, said of his experience:

> After my first cancer, even the smallest joys in life took on a special meaning—watching a beautiful sunset, a hug from a child, a laugh with Dorothy. After my second and third cancers, the simple joys of life are everywhere and are boundless.

A young man who had just turned 30 made an appointment because he was very depressed and he said he knew the reason for his great sadness. His main goal in life and his top priority for how to live was to be a millionaire by the time he was 30 and he had fallen short of his goal—he had amassed only "$750,000.00 in liquid assets" by his thirtieth birthday. The failure to achieve his chosen life goal had led him to great despair. Maybe his priorities needed a little shifting. Shifts in priorities are common for persons who have faced major life crises. Perhaps the young man needed the somewhat frank, and perhaps a little harsh, advice from a marathon runner who had been treated for cancer. "It may sound brutal, but maybe everybody should have a little cancer to help change them."

Most of the survivors of a ship that sank some years ago reported that they no longer took life for granted, and three out of four indicated that they now made it a priority to live each day to the fullest (Joseph, Williams, & Yule, 1993). Such changed priorities are reflected in the experience of a highly placed executive who had a heart attack. He had been a collegiate athlete and had never been seriously ill a day in his life. The cardiac event changed him. After he was released from the hospital he altered his work schedule to spend more time with his children, aged three and six. The importance of corporate advancement was no longer the single most important focus of his life—his family was. These examples illustrate two typical changes in life priorities reported as part of the experience of posttraumatic growth: the increased significance of small and simple things in life, and the recognition of the importance of relationships formerly taken for granted.

For some people the encounter with trauma can make salient, as never before, that everyday experiences and relationships are important, and maybe should be given higher priority. Tradition says that St. Francis of Assisi was once asked what he would do if he knew he had only one more day to live. "I would continue to hoe my garden," he responded. People who have experienced extremely trying circumstances may alter the way they view life and what they see as the most important elements in it. Like St. Francis, what they may come to realize is that, if life is indeed short and we as humans are vulnerable to significant losses, perhaps mindfully hoeing the garden is one of the most important things we can choose to do.

Herman (1992, p. 94) suggested that many persons exposed to traumatic events "experience the bitterness of being forsaken by God." This phrase aptly describes the experience of some persons, and perhaps at least the temporary experience of most persons who undergo major crises and loss. Even for atheists and agnostics Herman's phrase expresses a metaphorical sense of the desolation that some persons feel in the aftermath of trauma. For other persons, however, the confrontation with a traumatic event can provide the context for significant change in the existential sphere, change that the individual regards as positive and perhaps highly significant.

Ashlee F. was a woman in her thirties whose husband of three years was killed during a botched late-night robbery at a fast food restaurant. He, along with two others, had been taken hostage by the robber, but he was murdered by the criminal when the police made a surprise attempt at a rescue. Some months later, when talking about her experience to her therapist, Ashlee indicated that the murder of her husband had produced a crisis of faith for her, shaking the foundations of her religious beliefs and raising many questions about them. She also indicated that since his death she had experienced a sense of being in touch with something transcendent that was somehow comforting, but which she had difficulty putting into words. She was reluctant to use the traditional religious language of her faith, because "I am not sure the God I believed in really ever existed." Religious questions about what she believed and considered true remained unanswered. At the same time, her sense of being connected to something spiritual or transcendent was stronger and in some ways clearer than before her tragic loss.

The metaphor of the *thin places* (Gomes, 1996) provides one way of looking at the experience of spiritual or existential growth reported by some persons who encounter major suffering and challenge in life. In Celtic mythology the thin places are locations where the barrier between this world and "the other" is thinner and more permeable, allowing for the possibility of connecting more directly to that "other" world. From this point of view, such places are geographic locations. According to tradition, for example, the Isle of Iona, off the coast of Scotland, is one of those "thin places."

For some people, the experience of a major life crisis can represent a metaphorical thin place, where the confrontation with suffering or mortality makes them more aware of spiritual things, or makes them more likely to engage with the fundamental existential questions of meaning in life. For some of those, their experience happens within a traditional theistic belief system. This is often the case of the persons we have talked with in the South of the United States, a region where many people have traditional views of God and where many adhere to various versions of traditional Christianity. It is important to keep in mind, however, that *persons dealing with crisis in a traditionally religious way do not necessarily experience religious growth as an increase in the orthodoxy of their beliefs*. Their experience of growth may retain its religious meaning, but their specific beliefs may change in ways that represent a departure from orthodoxy and away from the acceptance of beliefs they may have had originally. But the change to a less traditional form of believing can represent a change to a deeper and more satisfying way of thinking and of living, even as it retains some of the original elements of religious belief.

It is important not to equate the metaphor of the thin places with an exclusively religious meaning. Even atheists or agnostics may experience their encounter with loss or trauma as an existential thin place. Their confrontation is not with questions about God or the religious meaning of suffering, but about the fundamental existential questions that are not limited to religious world views. Questions such as: What should I do with the rest of my life?; What sense can I make out of what is happening and will happen?; and What purpose, if any, is there to all this?

For some people, then, the encounter with trauma leads them to confront questions of meaning and purpose which may not have been salient before. For some persons, wrestling with those questions in the thin place of suffering and distress leads them to experiences and to understandings in the religious, spiritual, or purely existential realm, that can be deeply significant.

In Summary

The view that people can be changed, sometimes in radical ways, by their encounter with major challenges and with suffering is not new, but the systematic investigation of this phenomenon is relatively recent. Beginning with pioneering scholars in the mid-twentieth century, and with a variety of studies later in the century, posttraumatic growth is now a phenomenon being studied in many countries.

The experience of growth arising from the struggle with traumatic events is rather common. It has been reported, in at least some ways, by persons encountering a wide array of different situations (Calhoun & Tedeschi, 2006; Weiss &

Berger, 2010). Common elements of the experience include a changed sense of self, a change in the experience of one's relationships, and a changed philosophy of life. The change in self-perception may include an increased sense of vulnerability, but also an increased experience of oneself as capable of surviving suffering and of dealing with subsequent major problems in life. Positive changes in relationships can include a deepening of relationships with important others, a greater sense of compassion and sympathy for others who suffer, and a greater freedom of truthfully expressing oneself to others. Finally, some people report a greater appreciation for life, a changed sense in priorities, and meaningful changes in religious, spiritual or existential elements of their lives.

Individual and Event Specific Experiences

These three broad areas of posttraumatic growth represent the common core of the experience for persons facing a wide variety of specific challenges. However, a particular person may report specific changes that are not included in these categories. For example, persons diagnosed with cancer may report an increased commitment to living a healthier life, or a person who has been faced with the sexual infidelity of a trusted partner may report an increased focus on open and clear communication with other people they are close to. Clinicians will do well to be open to hearing reports of these specific kinds of changes; however, the broad areas of growth described above will serve as a useful general way of understanding what clients may experience and report.

But Please Remember

It is important to remember that not all persons who face tragedy and suffering experience posttraumatic growth. Some experience not one single element of posttraumatic growth and clinicians must remind themselves of that truth. This book is focused on posttraumatic growth in clinical work, but it is important to remember this. Depending on what the criteria are, a rough estimate is that between 30 percent to 90 percent of persons dealing with major difficulties report at least some elements of growth (Calhoun & Tedeschi, 2006). *Posttraumatic growth is common, but it is by no means universal.* In addition, there are some circumstances where the consideration that growth may be possible might be regarded by trauma survivors as naïve. It is not our intent to suggest that growth is a facile consequence of a bit of stress.

Life crises can have many negative consequences and for most people that is the norm rather than the exception. Even resilient persons, who in some situations represent the majority, probably experience varying degrees of distress of varying amounts of duration. What we are suggesting to clinicians is that when people face difficult life circumstances, some persons say that their struggle has changed them for the better, that they have grown as persons. Clinicians who work with clients who have faced trauma may find that some of them report posttraumatic growth. But are these reports of posttraumatic growth valid?

Are Reports of Posttraumatic Growth Reliable and Trustworthy?

Although it is something of an artificial distinction, it seems practical to address the question from two points of view. The purely scientific, research oriented perspective, where the primary concerns are with data and numbers, and a clinical perspective, where the point of reference is what clients tell clinicians about their lives and experiences.

Focus on the Research Setting

A key element for researchers is the accuracy and validity of self-reports gathered through the use of especially constructed inventories, such as the Stress-Related Growth Scale (Park, Cohen, & Murch, R), the Changes in Outlook Questionnaire (Joseph, Williams, & Yule, 1993), and the Posttraumatic Growth Inventory (PTGI) (Tedeschi and Calhoun, 1996). We will focus on the PTGI as an example of concerns about the trustworthiness of responses on inventories designed to assess growth. There are two broad ways of addressing the question: are these reports reliable and are they valid?

The answer to the first question is that self-reports of growth are reliable. The internal consistency of the PTGI, as well as its test-retest reliability, are good to excellent (Anderson & Lopez-Baez, 2008; Tedeschi & Calhoun, 1996). When responding to the scale, people tend to answer different questions within the inventory in a consistent way, and they give similar responses when asked the same questions at two different points in time. But even though the responses are reliable, are they trustworthy?

One way the validity of self-reports can be challenged is by indications that the responses reflect a bias toward making oneself "look good," that is, a tendency to respond to items on the scale in a socially desirable way. What does the research evidence indicate about the role of social desirability biases in self-reports of growth? The evidence is rather clear. Social desirability does not appear to be a factor in the answers people give on inventories that measure posttraumatic growth (Salsman, Segerstrom, Brechting, Carlson, & Andrykowski, 2009; Wild & Paivio, 2003).

Another way of asking about the trustworthiness of self-ratings of growth scales is to inquire as to whether or not those self-reports of growth reflect "genuine" or "actual" growth (Gunty, Frazier, Tennen, Tomich, Tashiro, & Park, 2010). One way of trying to answer this question is to evaluate the degree to which the self-reports are corroborated by others. When asked about what changes they have seen in the person directly affected by the critical event, for example, a person who has cancer, do others tend to report seeing the same changes that target persons report about themselves? The answer is yes. Self-reports of posttraumatic growth are reliably correlated with what others report seeing in the person making those assertions (Moore *et al.* 2011; Shakespeare-Finch & Enders, 2008; Weiss, 2002).

In general, then, reports of growth obtained on carefully developed measures of growth appear to be reliable and trustworthy (Aspinwall & Tedeschi, 2010). However, these scales tend to ask persons to consider changes that have occurred over time and the content of the items tends to be positive. Because of this, and in spite of the reasonably good support for the reliability and validity of scales such as the PTGI, at least one measure of growth has been developed that also allows respondents to indicate when they have experienced negative outcomes *in the same five domains of growth* described above. The resulting measure has not been in widespread use, but early indications are that people tend to report many more positive outcomes than negative ones (Baker, Kelly, Calhoun, Cann, & Tedeschi, 2008).

In contrast to the group averages that are typically evaluated in quantitative studies of the measurement properties of growth scales, it is probably wise to approach the scores of individuals with some degree of caution. The available data do suggest that for use with groups, where data from many different persons are combined, scales such as the PTGI do a good job of measuring what they were intended to measure in a reliable and valid way. When looking at the scores of one person, however, it is probably wise to interpret them with some degree of caution, keeping in mind that human beings do have a tendency toward self-enhancing biases that could possibly affect responses of one single individual, in ways that they may not affect the average scores of large groups of respondents. Furthermore, large degrees of reported change on particular items on the PTGI may indicate a quite significant personal experience for an individual, even though their overall score on the measure may be low.

Focus on Clinical Settings

Some researchers have appropriately raised the question about the validity of self-report measures of posttraumatic growth (Frazier, Tennen, Gavian, Park, Tomich, & Tashiro, 2009). Although, at least as we have interpreted it above, the research evidence generally supports the validity and reliability of measures such as the Posttraumatic Growth Inventory, this is an important question and additional studies will add new evidence. To some extent, this is an academic issue for persons whose primary focus is on statistical research with groups of people. Clinicians, however, are faced with specific accounts of growth in the context of their work with specific individuals, families, or groups. How should clinicians respond to reports of posttraumatic growth in the context of their work with survivors of traumatic events?

In this book we will often refer to the question of how to respond to themes of growth in a clinical context, so the answer for now will be brief and incomplete.

Our inclination is to recommend that clinicians respond to reports of posttraumatic growth nonjudgmentally, regarding them as part of that particular person's way of understanding what has happened to them, and as part of the narrative they are developing about their circumstances in particular and their lives in general (Neimeyer, 2006). Although clearly not a systematic study, in our combined clinical experience we have never encountered a single client whose descriptions of the growth they experienced from their struggle with suffering reflected significant levels of self-enhancing distortions. That certainly does not rule out the possibility that such biases can be at play, but this is a concern that we regard as important from the point of view of scientific inquiry about reports of growth, but a concern that is quite unlikely to be relevant in the routine practice of most clinicians working with survivors of major life crises. *We tend to simply accept as genuine the reports of growth that our clients make.* But what is the process through which the experience of growth occurs?

Understanding the Process of Posttraumatic Growth in Clinical Work

What factors are at work as the experience of posttraumatic growth unfolds? The most important factors that seem to be at play are summarized in Figure 1. This discussion will focus on elements that are relevant to working with clients, rather than on abstract issues that have relevance primarily for scientific inquiry.

The model of growth begins with characteristics of the person before the crisis situation occurs. Personality characteristics, such as extraversion or openness to experience, may influence the likelihood of subsequent growth (Shakespeare-Finch, Gow, & Smith, 2005). The individual's gender may also affect the possibility of growth, with women showing a somewhat greater tendency to report posttraumatic growth (Vishnevsky, Cann, Calhoun, Tedeschi, & Demakis, 2010). A very important factor influencing the possibility that growth will be experienced is the individual's assumptive world (Janoff-Bulman, 1992; Parkes, 1971), the general set of beliefs a person has about the universe, how it works, and the individual's place in it. *As we view them, traumatic events are those that have a seismic impact on the individual's assumptive world.* Just like an earthquake can shake, damage, or destroy physical structures, traumatic events have the same kind of impact on the schemas and beliefs people use to help them understand and organize their experiences.

Some events can lead people to review or question their fundamental beliefs about the world and their place in it; this process of reviewing and examining core beliefs is a key catalyst for the subsequent possibility of posttraumatic growth (Cann, Calhoun, Tedeschi, Triplett, Vishnevsky, & Lindstrom, 2010). As the model indicates, this examination of core beliefs, precipitated by the major stressor, is a key element that can set the stage for growth. For persons whose assumptive world provides a context for, and a full understanding of the event, there is no challenge to core beliefs, and there will be little or no posttraumatic

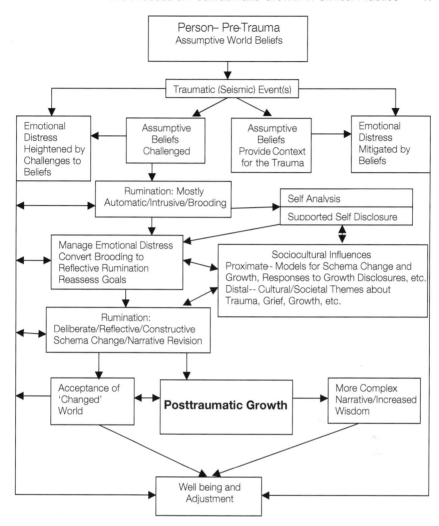

Figure 1.1 A Model of Posttraumatic Growth (Lawrence Calhoun, Richard Tedeschi & Arnie Cann)

growth engendered by the confrontation with major stressors. The difficult circumstances may produce emotional distress, but they are unlikely to initiate a process leading to growth. Persons who hold views such as "God is in control," or "Everything unfolds according to a divine plan," for example, are not likely to have those core beliefs challenged or threatened, and neither are persons who assume that life is unpredictable and that events occur randomly. These broad assumptions cannot be invalidated by life circumstances and they are not likely to be contradicted by events, no matter how tragic.

However, when the set of circumstances does lead to significant challenge to core beliefs, then the stage is set for possible posttraumatic growth. The challenge or disruption of the assumptive world, which can also be associated with the disruption of important goals or of one's life narrative, is likely to produce significant rumination. Rumination, repeatedly thinking about the same sorts of things, involves cognitive work that is precipitated by the disruption or challenge to important core beliefs. In the early days of the crisis situation, rumination is likely to have an intrusive quality; people may think about their situation even when they do not want to do so. In this context, however, it is important to remember that this very interest in, and perhaps need for, repeated thinking is also a trait on which people differ (Silvia, 2011). Some people do not want or need to think about things to try to reach some kind of resolution. For many people, the question of "why me" never comes up. This general view may also be part of the individual's assumptive world reflected in the general belief that "there is just no sense in thinking about stuff a lot in order to try to figure things out." Within the clinical context, however, it is probably useful to approach clients with the view that repeated thinking about the event and its ramifications is typical.

With the passage of some amount of time, repeated thinking about what has happened, and perhaps how to try to comprehend it, can develop a more deliberate quality. This form of rumination can be reflective, deliberate, and focused on making sense of events (Martin & Tesser, 1996). This more deliberate form of rumination appears to be particularly important for the possibility of subsequent growth (Cann, Calhoun, Tedeschi, Triplett, Vishnevsky, & Lindstrom, 2011; Stockton, Hunt, & Joseph, 2011).

Early in the posttraumatic journey the individual may be overwhelmed with emotional distress, and clinicians need to focus on that element before any consideration of the possibility of posttraumatic growth is undertaken. As coping or treatment help reduce overwhelming emotional distress, rumination that is more deliberate may begin to replace more intrusive forms, making the possibility of subsequent growth more likely.

Clinicians need to understand as much as they can about their clients' social contexts (see Chapter 3) and this understanding is also relevant to understanding the possibility of growth arising from the struggle with trauma. *The person's experience in the posttraumatic world occurs within a complicated set of interacting sociocultural influences and the model reflects some of this complexity.* The difficult event can lead to cognitive engagement with core beliefs and to rumination and distress, and those can in turn lead some persons to engage in what we might call self-analysis, through repeated thinking, or writing about, or perhaps sharing one's experiences with other persons.

The presence of supportive others, particularly those who maintain support for as long as it is requested or needed, can play an important role in the individual's process of coping with traumatic events (Wilcox, 2010). With regard to growth, it is likely that the availability of growth themes in both the person's proximate and distal cultures, as well as the ways in which growth is understood, modeled, and reinforced or sanctioned, can affect the individual's experience of growth. A very large proportion of a sample of university students in the Southern United States, for example, reported having encountered themes of posttraumatic growth in their own sociocultural contexts (Lindstrom, Cann, Calhoun, & Tedeschi, 2011). In addition, the way people are willing to report positive changes, and the kinds of changes that are viewed as reflecting growth, can vary with the particular cultural setting (Taku, 2011).

Socio-cultural themes and understandings of growth may in turn influence the degree to which others will respond with social acceptance or with social approbation when an individual reveals the experience of some form of posttraumatic growth. In cultural settings where a collectivist view prevails, and perhaps where disclosures about one's successes or positive qualities are considered socially inappropriate, one might expect people to be less likely to disclose to others their experience of growth, and such disclosures might be more likely to be met with social disapproval. When cultural forces encourage the experience of posttraumatic growth the individual might be expected to be more open to such possibilities, might be more likely to engage in self-disclosure regarding that experience and, when receiving positive social responses to such disclosure, might be more likely to experience some form of posttraumatic growth.

Posttraumatic Growth Beyond the Individual

We also recognize that social forces are involved in the process of posttraumatic growth in another way. Tragic events may be jointly experienced within a family, community, or even a nation. Just as these jointly experienced events can lead to major disruptions in the functioning of the group, it appears that they may also lead to posttraumatic growth that is shared among people. Weiss (2002) has documented this shared growth among breast cancer survivors and their husbands, and we have previously discussed examples of how this may be seen in bereaved parents (Tedeschi & Calhoun, 2004).

Beyond these experiences within families, there can also be a determination by communities to address tragedy by attempting to create a positive outcome. For example, in Tucson, Arizona, one year after the shooting of several people, including Congresswoman Gabrielle Giffords, her Rabbi, Stephanie Aaron said "Even in the midst of this troubling year, the healing, the courage that we have experienced in our community—each one of us can notice how our cups overflow with the blessings of our lives" (Myers, 2012). In such attempts to heal communities in the aftermath of violence, natural disaster, or other traumas, clinicians may play a role in individual and community responses. But generally, the responses are determined by many individuals in the community and their leaders. One of the growth outcomes in such situations may be that individuals transform themselves into leaders in their attempts to help their neighbors. Entire societies may be transformed as well as individuals, as social movements and political change can result from catastrophe. Some examples of such changes are Japan after World War II, or South Africa post-Apartheid (Bloom, 1998; Solnit, 2009; Tedeschi, 1999).

Posttraumatic Growth and Optimal Psychological Functioning

The question about whether or not posttraumatic growth is related to general psychological adjustment is a puzzling one. If people see themselves as stronger than they thought possible, or feel a greater degree of closeness and intimacy with others, or have a better-developed and more satisfying philosophy of life, asking them a question that amounts to "So, what?" seems a bit insulting, and perhaps silly. But, the question regarding the degree to which the experience of growth is, or is not, related to other areas of psychological functioning is one that researchers, and perhaps clinicians, would like answered.

One question asked about the experience of growth is whether reports of growth are related to other measures of psychological functioning, particularly emotional distress or well-being. Studies that have examined the relationship between posttraumatic growth, on the one hand, and psychological distress or well-being, on the other, are mixed. One possible reason for this inconsistency is the influence of cultural factors (Shakespeare-Finch & Morris, 2010). Much of the available evidence, however, suggests that it may be more accurate, and perhaps more useful clinically, to regard the experience of growth and the experience of psychological pain and distress as independent dimensions; changes in one will not necessarily be related to changes in the other. In other words, these two general domains, distress and growth, are best viewed as independent outcomes of the influence of highly challenging events and of the person's struggles to come to terms with them.

Some evidence indicates that growth may have an impact more generally, for example, on life satisfaction, but the influence may be indirect. One variable that appears to be involved in the relationship between life satisfaction and growth is the presence of meaning in one's life (Linley & Joseph, 2011). One study has suggested that reports of posttraumatic growth have a reliable influence on the presence of meaning in life, which in turn influences the overall level of life satisfaction (Triplett, Tedeschi, Cann, Calhoun, & Reeve, 2012). Persons who experience growth are more likely to report lives that have purpose and meaning, and meaning in turn is likely to be connected to higher levels of general life satisfaction.

Our model of growth also suggests that the experience of posttraumatic growth is closely tied to people's narratives about their lives generally and the event in particular. For some persons, the event becomes a central focus of identity, something that can have both good and bad consequences (Schuettler & Boals, 2011). For persons who regard the struggle with the difficult circumstances as a positive turning point in life, that led, for example, to a clearer philosophy of life or to an enhanced sense of purpose in life, then the growth component of the narrative can clarify and enhance the life story. However, persons who regard the event as a defining negative turning point in their life stories, and who focus on its typical negative consequences, may have significant dissatisfaction with life and perhaps significant psychological distress. Although a bit simple, the distinction can be made between these two kinds of broad interpretations of traumatic events. Does the person now think of the life narrative as the story of a wounded victim, or the story of a strong survivor? Those whose experience of growth leads them to see themselves as survivors, who have struggled with a difficult set of circumstances but who somehow prevailed and grew, will likely develop a more adaptive life narrative (Groleau, Calhoun, Cann, & Tedeschi, in press).

It can also be useful to view the experience of the encounter with trauma, the subsequent struggles to cope with the consequences, and the possible experience of posttraumatic growth, as connected to greater life wisdom. There has been surprisingly little scholarly investigation of the connection of these factors (Linley, 2003), but from a clinical point of view it seems useful to consider the possibility of their interrelatedness. The struggle with a major life crisis can lay the foundation for the possibility of growth, but it may also encourage the development of life wisdom (Ardelt, 2003; Baltes & Smith, 2008). As individuals face life in the aftermath of suffering and loss, there may be an opportunity for the experience of posttraumatic growth, and also for the development of ways of living that are perhaps deeper and wiser.

Does Posttraumatic Growth Contribute to "Happiness"?

The proposed model of growth has as its endpoint, psychological well-being and life satisfaction. The prevailing contemporary view of human well-being, particularly among psychologists in the United States in the 21st century, has tended to focus on the goal of helping people generally, and clients in particular, achieve states of subjective well-being characterized by the presence of positive, and the absence of negative, affect (Ryan & Deci, 2001). An alternative, and somewhat more comprehensive view of human well-being, follows the view originally developed by the ancient Greek philosopher Aristotle. Aristotle argued that the primary function of human life was to achieve what he called *eudaimonia,* a word that describes the state of flourishing as a human being—to fully realize one's possibilities for living a full life. Our view is more in keeping with this Aristotelian view, which has much in common with the general ideas of the humanistic psychologists of the mid-twentieth century, who regarded self-actualization as the most desirable manifestation of human flourishing (Rogers, 1961). *Posttraumatic growth is not necessarily an experience that leads people to feel less pain from tragedies they have experienced, nor does it necessarily lead to an increase in positive emotions.* As we have suggested, it may be useful for clinicians to regard growth and distress as independent dimensions. Growth can contribute to a recognition of what is important in living well and fully, but it will not necessarily lead, at least not directly, to an increase in a subjective sense of feeling cheerful.

There may well be circumstances where the hard-won experience of growth, and perhaps a more meaningful life narrative and an increase in life wisdom, will not be accompanied by a commensurate lessening of the pain of loss. But the experience of growth is reflected in the sense that one's priorities have been reordered in a more desirable way, where life, even in its simple pleasures, is more deeply appreciated, where one's connections with significant others have become closer and deeper, and where one's own personal answers to the central questions of life now have clearer and more satisfying answers.

Note

1   Here, we use the terms *trauma, crisis, major stressor,* and related terms as essentially synonymous expressions to describe very difficult circumstances that significantly challenge or invalidate important components of the person's assumptive world.

two
Facilitating Posttraumatic Growth through Expert Companionship

The process of posttraumatic growth that we have described in Chapter 1 is usually a naturally occurring one, not assisted by professionals, but instead it evolves from survivors' ways of coping, thinking about their disrupted belief systems, and through interactions with their natural social environments. But some people do come to the attention of health professionals as they deal with the psychological and, in many cases, the physical difficulties that major stressors can cause. Professionals then have the opportunity to nurture the processes that tend to promote recuperation and perhaps posttraumatic growth. It has been extremely rare for any trauma survivor to present him or herself to us with the request for us to help them develop posttraumatic growth. On a rare occasion, we have had people say, "I want to make something good come out of all this" but more often people are simply trying to find a way to manage the misery they are experiencing in the aftermath of trauma.

We call the stance we take as professionals in helping people who are coming to us for assistance in coping with trauma and its aftermath *expert companionship* (Tedeschi & Calhoun, 2006). The term emphasizes the view that both professional expertise and human companionship are crucial for the people seeking our help. This stance can be crucial in facilitating the process of posttraumatic growth. We choose these words we use carefully; we see ourselves as *facilitators* rather than creators of growth, *companions* who offer some *expertise* in nurturing naturally occurring processes of healing and growth. Just as we can think of many of the procedures that physicians perform on the body as facilitating a healing process that the body must ultimately do for itself, we see ourselves as likewise facilitating a healing process that is psychological. In trauma survivors, the injuries are often so great that this process is too disturbed or challenged to function smoothly, so our job as professionals is to help it work more effectively. In this chapter we will review various aspects of the facilitation that the expert companion provides. We will describe the kind of companionship we seek to give to trauma survivors, and the various aspects of expertise that is necessary to address the tasks that appear to be important in moving toward a growth outcome.

Companionship First

In a recent meeting of several hundred military service members the concept of posttraumatic growth was described, and then the audience was polled to see how many had experienced this themselves or had known someone else who had experienced it. Almost 90 percent indicated that they had seen posttraumatic growth in themselves or others. Then they were asked if they had ever needed an expert companion. Almost 70 percent reported that they had and those companions had been either friends or family. Only about 10 percent were helped by professionals. The companionship survivors of trauma need is most often provided by those in their environment who are convenient and easily accessible, or most trusted, and not often by professionals who are harder to find and with whom the trauma survivors have no prior relationship. Perhaps as professionals we would do well to try to emulate the best aspects of the relationships trauma survivors have with these helpful companions.

We use the term *companion* to emphasize that simply *being with* a survivor of trauma who is experiencing misery and confusion can bring significant comfort to this person. A good clinician leads with companionship rather than technical expertise or knowledge. The clinician recognizes that navigating trauma situations is not merely an intellectual exercise but instead involves much emotion. Especially in the early phases of helping trauma survivors the expertise that trauma clinicians offer should be expertise in relating and listening. Being a comforting presence for people who are trying to figure out how to be a trauma survivor is a basic skill without which any other knowledge of trauma processes or intervention strategies becomes almost pointless.

A family sought help to deal with the tragic suicidal death of the mother. A woman of 50, she had committed suicide after living for a year with a painful illness. The husband had found her in their garage with the car engine running when he came home from work. He and their two children in their twenties, were shocked, saddened, and confused. What could the clinician offer? A month after this event, should the counselor tell them that they would feel better in the future? Offer ways to obtain the "closure" that reporters on the local news talk about in such circumstances? Tell them they need to help each other? Tell them they shouldn't feel guilty and are not to blame? The clinician chose to do very little other than show interest in their story, allow himself to feel what this might be like for them, given the particulars of their family and the circumstances, and let them know he would like to offer them what help he could.

When we are training our graduate students in the basic skills of interviewing and psychotherapy, we often find that they are dismayed by the kind of approach taken with this family. The message we often hear boils down to something like "Is that all?" Of course, this is only a start, but it is a way of relating to trauma survivors that should carry through all the work that is done. It is starting from the particular place of this family or this person, understanding their environment, their language, their emotional needs, their beliefs and their confusion about what has happened to them. This way of relating is fundamental and has been described by many psychologists over the decades. Yet it seems we need to continue to relearn the lessons.

Theodore Reik (1948) taught clinicians to "listen with the third ear" or the part of the clinician that reacts to the subtleties of clients' presentations that evoke emotional reactions, associations, and intuitions in the clinician. Carl Rogers (1957) described the "necessary and sufficient conditions" for therapeutic change that include empathy, genuineness and unconditional positive regard. George Kelly (1969) encouraged clinicians to mute their intellectual analysis of meaning and listen instead to the "subcortical sounds" and "preverbal outcries" contained in clients' talk. Listening to clients in these open, accepting ways forms the basis for clearly understanding and relating, and this is what can make so much difference in the success of our efforts. This is clearly shown in the research findings about the power of effective therapy relationships, or therapeutic alliance (Norcross & Wampold, 2011). Being the kind of companion who is focused on the nuances of the trauma survivor in a way that extends beyond the intellectual to the personal is so fundamental that we can find the same principles guiding work with animals. Horse trainer Monty Roberts (1999), for example, describes a process of "joining-up" with wild and abused horses that involves a gentle invitation to connect by understanding and responding to the messages in the horses' behavior. He spent much time observing horses and learning the subtleties of their communication. He is essentially an equine trauma therapist who practices the same fundamental principles of relating that we see as necessary in working with human trauma survivors.

Expert companions are interested in learning about the trauma survivors they meet, but more than that, learning *from* them. Expert companions recognize that they are, in many ways, in the same boat as our clients. We can be struck by trauma at any time, or perhaps already have been. From this perspective on our mutual human condition, we seek to learn about what it is like to go through what trauma survivors go through. Taking the stance that we are going to be learning from our clients, rather than teaching them or treating them, may seem to be an odd approach in these days where as clinicians we find ourselves "providers of healthcare services" who must submit "treatment plans" into electronic medical records. But paradoxically, when we allow ourselves to learn the language of trauma survivors, empathize with their worldviews that may now be in shambles, and to tolerate not only hearing about, but feeling some of the impact of the story of their suffering, we are creating the circumstances where the best trauma treatment will be accomplished. In this kind of treatment, trauma survivors find not only relief from many symptoms, but a way of living that holds great value despite the facts of the trauma, and some enduring distress.

Growth oriented trauma treatment that expert companions practice extends beyond a goal of removing certain symptoms such as sleep problems, anxiety reactions, suspiciousness, irritability, distractibility, or the like. The expert companion is intent on appreciating the experience of the trauma survivor in such a way that the person can feel emotionally safe enough to explore all that is going on in their situation, and therefore not have to waste effort on keeping memories, feelings, or thoughts secret from the therapist or out of their own awareness. With this ability to more fully experience their trauma situation possibilities for personal change develop. Trauma survivors become willing to consider the memories, feelings and thoughts that may be embarrassing, or seem dangerous. This gives the clinician a chance to provide some perspective on these experiences. Being an expert companion also allows you to become much more knowledgeable about the trauma experience, so that with future clients you will be able to apply this knowledge by sharing some of the things that have been discovered by people who have gone through similar circumstances or faced similar challenges.

Being respectful, by listening to trauma survivors' stories patiently and seeking to understand their viewpoints, enables you to gain the respect of these clients. Expert companions are willing to listen to the worst aspects of people's stories: the gruesome parts, the ways they feel crazy, the embarrassing things, and the things they feel guilty about. By not shying away from such topics, expert companions become appreciated, because so many others in trauma survivors' lives cannot tolerate these stories, are made uncomfortable by them, or get tired of hearing them.

Expert Companionship and PTG in Evidence-based Trauma Treatment

Facilitation of PTG can be accomplished by implementing the principles we describe here within commonly practiced evidence-based trauma treatment. Only recently have trauma treatments begun to incorporate elements of PTG theory and practice (e.g. Meichenbaum, 2006; Zoellner & Maercker, 2006), but existing standard treatments can be adapted to focus on possibilities for growth. When focused only on the need to identify and address the negative conse-quences of major life crises, clinicians may inadvertently overlook the possibility that some, perhaps many, individuals can experience positive change in the wake of tragedy and loss. We encourage clinicians to move beyond an exclusive focus on the negative, to seeing strength and the possibility of growth as well.

There are a variety of therapeutic approaches to trauma (Shapiro, 2010), based on varying therapeutic principles, and that may be individual, group, inpatient, outpatient, brief, and long-term treatment (Wilson, Friedman, & Lindy, 2001).

Evidence-based treatments for trauma include several approaches that have common elements (Foa, Keane, Terence, Friedman, & Cohen, 2009; Sharpless & Barber, 2011). Prolonged Exposure (PE) (Foa, Hembree, & Rothbaum, 2007) is typically delivered in eight to ten weekly 90-minute sessions of imaginal revisiting of trauma memories, recounting them aloud and discussing them immediately afterward. Also, *in vivo* versions of PE are sometimes attempted. Cognitive Processing Therapy (CPT) (Resick & Schnicke, 1993; Monson, Schnurr, Resick, Friedman, Young-Xu, & Stevens, 2006) has also been provided as a brief therapy of approximately 12 sessions with a writing exposure format where clients read their accounts daily as well as during sessions. Accounts include sensory memories, feelings and thoughts. Cognitive-behavioral therapy (CBT) aspects of this approach include labeling feelings and working through stuck points, such as self-blame. These CBT aspects appear to be more powerful than the exposure component of this treatment. Eye Movement Desensitization and Reprocessing (EMDR) (Shapiro, 2005) includes elements of CBT and mindfulness approaches. Unique phases of treatment involve tracking moving fingers of the therapist while holding distressing images or positive cognitions in mind. Results of studies of EMDR appear similar to or less effective than exposure-based therapies (Taylor, 2003), and the novel aspects do not seem to add much to outcome (Cusack & Spates, 1999; Davidson & Parker, 2001). Stress Inoculation Training (SIT) includes relaxation, thought-stopping and *in vivo* exposure, and it has some limited evidence of efficacy (Cahill, Rothbaum, Resick, & Follette, 2009). Cognitive-Exposure Therapy with Virtual Reality (VR) is a new treatment modality that has become possible with the advent of sophisticated computer simulation. It includes convincing visual stimuli, sound, and smells in the simulations of trauma experiences. It may be preferred by those unwilling to consider traditional treatment, and recent studies support its efficacy (Sharpless & Barber, 2011).

These standard evidence-based trauma treatments tend to have common elements. One element, exposure with desensitization, is important in trauma treatment. Because the events surrounding the traumatic event, and what has become associated with it provoke anxiety in the form of exaggerated startle responses, hypervigilance and the like, and avoidance responses that have both behavioral and cognitive elements, desensitization has become a common aspect of all trauma treatment. This is accomplished through exposure to the trauma in detailed descriptions or thinking of traumatic events in conjunction with a safe therapeutic atmosphere, directed eye movements, hypnotic or relaxation procedures, and so on. Of course, psychopharmacological interventions are often useful in alleviating many of these symptoms (Sharpless & Barber, 2011). In providing exposure treatment, expert companionship is crucial because exposure is such an anxiety-arousing experience. Many survivors of major stressors resist therapy that involves exposure, so being with an expert companion who clearly understands the psychological risks involved for these clients can make a big difference in willingness to engage in this aspect of trauma treatment.

A second element of trauma treatment involves understanding the circumstances surrounding the events and drawing conclusions about them that will answer questions about what happened, how and why these things happened, who might be responsible, and how things will be different as a result. The traumatic events themselves and the impact of the events are scrutinized. The impact of the ways the survivor is coping with the events should also be carefully considered. The cognitive processing of these issues can take some time and can lead to the creation of a coherent narrative of the trauma and the aftermath. The narrative makes sense of the incidents or at least makes them understandable in some basic way. Because traumatic events are often poorly encoded in memory, a narrative serves the purpose of linking together elements of traumatic memories, speculations about motives of those involved, and other aspects of the trauma so that the survivor has a good enough model to refer to in recovery. Trauma survivors must have some degree of clarity about what they are recovering from. An expert companion allows clients to carefully examine the thinking processes involved in considering the events and their impact.

A third important element of trauma treatment is the recreation of a sense of safety. This can arise out of exposure and desensitization, and the understanding of the crisis event and the aftermath. Expert companionship plays an important role in the development of a sense of safety. This happens in the therapeutic alliance and also at times through making connections with other trauma survivors. The therapeutic goal is to replace extreme strategies of avoidance with better self-protective strategies that allow trauma survivors to feel less vulnerable.

Final Steps in PTG: Moving into the Narrative, Constructivist, and Existential Realms of Therapy

A final element that is important is trauma treatment involves the rebuilding of a worldview that encompasses what happened, as well as a functional life post trauma. To some extent, this aspect of trauma treatment involves the reconstruction of the narrative that describes the traumatic circumstances, and provides some understanding of it. The new assumptive world should also allow for a more hopeful stance toward the future, including how a survivor could be free of distressing symptoms, how life might be possible without revictimization, and how meaning and purpose are still possible. PTG can be a central element in this aspect of trauma therapy. At this point in facilitating PTG, the actions of the clinician incorporate concepts and approaches to therapy that emphasize the reconstruction of narrative, and the construction of meaning, elements that come into therapy when a sense of relative emotional safety has been established, emotional distress has been mitigated, and reflective, deliberate rumination or cognitive processing has been engaged. Perhaps the best known form of therapy that directs attention toward meaning is Frankl's (1988) logotherapy. Wong (2012) has elaborated on this approach with his meaning-centered counseling and therapy. Narrative approaches such as Neimeyer's (2006a, 2006b) grief therapy also focus on the development of a meaningful life narrative in the aftermath of loss.

As we describe how to be expert companions and how to utilize principles of PTG in trauma treatment, we will *not* be describing a new form of therapy, but how to maximize the effect of evidence-based trauma treatments, which tend to be cognitive-behavioral, and to extend their impact to more meaningful outcomes than symptom removal alone by integrating narrative/constructive and existential approaches. To have the maximum long-term impact, trauma treatment needs to promote the development of psychological resilience that allows people to withstand the situations that remind them of past traumas, and possible future traumatic events. This resilience is created out of a growth perspective in treatment that helps trauma survivors develop a revised set of core beliefs that allows them to make sense of what has happened to them, that are incorporated into a life narrative that guides their short- and long-term goals that have been adjusted in the aftermath of trauma (Wrosch, Scheier, Miller, & Carver, 2012) and allows events to seem understandable and meaningful. These internal structures of understanding and meaning become the central element in facilitating PTG through expert companionship.

The Very Beginning of Treatment: Incorporating Expert Companionship with a View Toward PTG

Clinicians in every profession have some training in the skill of accurately understanding the client's internal world (i.e., the process of empathy). The clinician must understand the client's general worldview and belief system. To enhance the possibility of PTG, the clinician must start the therapeutic work from within this framework. One specific area involves the acceptance and tolerance of "positive illusions" (Taylor & Brown, 1988, 1994). There is some evidence indicating that human beings tend to operate with certain benign illusions (Taylor, 1989). In the beginning of therapy, the expert companion is careful to respect these ideas, even if he or she notices that some of these ideas may need to be addressed later in the therapy. The expert companion who is attuned to simultaneously providing evidence-based trauma treatment and a growth oriented approach, will be paying attention to the negative aspects of the trauma survivor's experience, but also the strengths, capabilities, and possibilities for growth inherent in the early narrative that the trauma survivor recounts.

What follows is a first session with a survivor of an industrial accident. Although the expert companion appears to be simply listening to the story that is recounted, and not doing much to gather information, we can also realize that much is going on behind the scenes, as the clinician considers what is happening in the session in terms of PTG.

C (Client): They sent me here because I have been having trouble functioning since it happened. A guy I work with who was in 'Nam said I got PTSD. I thought you could only get that in war, but he said I am looking bad and I should get checked out. He went and talked to the manager which kind of pissed me off, but they're probably right.

Right away, the expert companion becomes aware of the ambivalence the client has about being helped. The way the coworker and manager handled this may not have been optimal. But the client did come to treatment and this presents an opportunity for a different way of providing help, and for the client to experience being helped.

T (Therapist): What happened?
C: You mean the accident?
T: Yeah.
C: Boiler exploded. It was awful. Ned was standing over on the platform next to it. It just happened so quick he didn't have a chance. It got me a little but it could have been worse.
T: I'm trying to imagine what this was like.

The therapist's statement represents an attempt to show that he very much wishes to put himself in the client's frame of experience. Instead of asking about particular details, he allows the client to focus on those things that may be most relevant to him.

C: It was unbelievable. Just blew with this huge sound and all this boiling water shooting over everything and these metal chunks launched at us. And then suddenly it's over and it's like what the fuck happened, and I've got these burns and I see Ned, and… and… well, I've never seen anything like it. I can't believe he was alive one minute and then like that… I just hate to think about it. But I do. I see it. Him, I mean.
T: It sounds horrific.

Notice how the story pours out of the client as he is given a chance to recount it. There is also the element of incredulity here. This event is bizarre and "unbelievable." But the most unbelievable element is that his coworker Ned was alive one moment and dead the next. This suggests already what the central focus of the client's ruminations might be, and what aspect of his assumptive world have been challenged. But it is time to just listen and get a clear understanding of the client's experience and how he has been trying to make sense of it. The expert companion is patient and reserves work on these issues for later.

C: It's messed me up.
T: The burns.

The clinician here recognizes the ambiguity of the comment "It's messed me up." Does it mean he has been physically messed up? Certainly, as the clinician can see his burned face. But of course there is already some indication that it has psychologically, emotionally, messed him up, seeing his coworker suddenly killed. But, it might be better to address the obvious things first, and in this way show that as an expert companion the clinician will not flinch from this or any other part of the experience.

C: Yeah, second and third degree. Besides this (points to one side of his face) it's on my chest and this arm. I look like hell, don't I?

The clinician does not answer this question. It may be a rhetorical question from the client or a statement that he thinks he looks like hell. But at this early stage, either agreeing with him or disagreeing may be a sign of lack of sensitivity, so maybe it is best to consider learning about another obvious aspect of the client's experience: pain.

T: Are you having pain from it?
C: Yeah, they had to do some grafting and stuff—I have more procedures to go. My face will likely never be right but it is better than it was. I'm not ever going to be my old beautiful self.

The comment from the client that he may never be his "old beautiful self" may demonstrate something important. It may be a sign that humor is an important coping mechanism for him. It may be an indication that he is concerned about the change in his appearance, and that this has been an important aspect of his identity. He may be trying to minimize this aspect of the aftermath of the trauma. It is also a way of talking about things the expert companion may need to be able to join with. So, the clinician will keep in mind that kidding around about things could be useful, but given the gravity of the trauma, he needs to make sure not to come across as dismissive. He can help the client use his humor in a constructive way, and integrate it into his identity post trauma.

T: What is the hardest part of all this?
C: You know, I'm learning to deal with the pain and operations better than you might think, I suppose. But it is real hard going back there to work.

This question about the impact of the trauma is an attempt to see what the client views as his greatest challenge. It is important to learn this from the client and to not make assumptions about what is difficult for a person. The expert companion learns from the client.

T: What happens?
C: I just keep seeing it all.

T: Images of what happened.
C: Bobby says they're flashbacks.
T: Your coworker from Vietnam?
C: Yeah. He's the expert he thinks.
T: He thinks.

In this exchange, the expert companion again turns to wanting to know about the client's experience. He also is leaving room for the client—notice the economy of language. Just a few words suffice. The implicit message is "This is about you—I want to hear your story and your experience. I am not going to get in the way or pretend I understand you." Also, the comment about Bobby the coworker thinking he is the "expert" can be taken as an instruction to the clinician about how this client will view attempts to show expertise. Expert *companionship* should be emphasized. The clinician subtly accepts the client's point of view on Bobby while asking a question in the form of a two word statement: "He thinks."

C: He acts like he knows all about what's going on cause he said he had PTSD after the war and he has all these vet buddies who have it, and he tells me stuff and I sometimes just don't want to hear it, I just want to shut this out and try to be normal again. But I pull into the parking lot and I start to get nervous and then I go in and I'll see the flashback of the explosion, and can hear it. And then I'll see what happened to Ned.

The client describes how his coworker may be trying to help but in the process is creating additional discomfort for him. The coworker is not an expert companion even though he may have good intentions. The client cannot go at the pace that Bobby is setting by providing the information on PTSD. An expert companion must join up with the client at this point in the struggle. Right now the client is struggling with intrusive images and anxiety, and just wishing he were not going through this.

T: What happened to Ned?
C: Pretty much decapitated.
T: What a terrible thing to see.
C: I heard a guy out in the shed talking about it last week. I was just going by and he was talking about it and kind of made fun of it—do you believe it? I first got really pissed. Then I felt sick. I went and threw up.
T: It's hard to handle this stuff.

The client states that he is having intrusive images about what happened to Ned, so the expert companion ventures into this part of the client's experience, by simply asking what happened to Ned. The simple response about decapitation belies how much this image is distressing to the client, and how central it is to his troubles. The expert companion gives simple reflections on how very difficult this whole thing is, implying that the client's responses to this event are understandable. The client also mentions overhearing a coworker making fun of Ned's decapitation. The client's sense of humor does not include this kind of insensitivity to Ned. This lack of sensitivity by the coworker in the shed literally makes the client sick. This may indicate that the client is a man who is sensitive and therefore he may be affected differently than the man in the shed. Also, he was a witness to it while the man in the shed may not have been, although that is not clear. Witnessing is different from hearing about an event. These are things the clinician is thinking about and storing for possible later use in the therapy. But the perspective of the expert companion who is wanting to facilitate PTG is that the client's reactions are not merely symptoms to be overcome, but indication of his humanity and sensitivity that could be better accepted and become clearer parts of his identity.

C: I should be over it. It was six months ago. I mean it was bad, but it's over. Why can't I just move on? My stupid brain won't let go of it. I've been thinking I should get another job—just get out of there. But I took a week's vacation, and I still thought about it. So it might just follow me. And jobs aren't easy to get. So, here I am with a shrink. No offense, but I think I've sunk pretty low.

These statements indicate a lack of technical understanding of how traumatic events may affect the brain and the mind. He calls his brain "stupid" and this indicates a need for some psychoeducation about trauma response. But he also recognizes that apparently simple solutions such as getting another job may not really work. He also indicates that the idea of seeing a 'shrink' bothers him, that the need for some professional help about this may indicate weakness.

T: Never been through anything like this?
C: Nothing has ever done this to me.
T: Are there other troubles this is causing you?

This is another question about the impact of the highly stressful events. In facilitating PTG the focus is on the aftermath of the trauma and how the person is coping, and not only the event itself.

C: Like I said I can deal with the operations and stuff now—it is painful but I can gut it out. I can deal with pain.
T: So the worst is what happens when you go to work?
C: Well, there's more, I guess.
T: What's that?
C: I don't even know how to talk about it. It's weird.
T: I'm listening—give it a try.

This lets the client know that the clinician will be a patient expert companion and he can just "give it a try" rather than have everything sorted out. The clinician

gets the notion from this that the client will need help articulating his experience or thought about it. This is part of the *expertise* an expert companion has—to help in the articulation of experience, and the bringing into awareness and disclosure the poorly understood aspect of the human response to trauma. So this is an exciting development in the conversation because the clinician may be in a position to allow the client to find out the value of expert companionship. The clinician may get to be more a companion, and less a "shrink."

> C: Well, it's like I keep thinking of Ned—here one minute gone the next. He was a really good guy—nice as can be, a happy sort, wife, three little kids he just thought the world of. A living guy, and then I see him, and he's just a corpse, all mangled. It's crazy.
> T: It doesn't make sense.
> C: This is bothering me. No—not bothering—more than that. It's like... I don't know even what to say about it. I just keep thinking how could he be here living his life and suddenly he is just a messed up... body... like, like... just meat.
> T: Makes you think.

The clinician continues to use very economical language that simply acknowledges how difficult it is to understand this experience. The clinician might have been tempted to focus on the thin line between life and death, and on philosophical ideas about mortality and such. But he would not be much of a companion. Instead, the expert companion stays close to the client's struggle with this traumatic experience. At some later point the client and clinician can collaborate to see if there is a way to make sense of what happened, to develop beliefs about it, and live a different life in the long-term aftermath of this. The above interchange also makes clear that the client is acutely aware of the impact of Ned's death on his family, another demonstration of the client's sensitivity.

> C: Yeah and not good stuff.
> T: Like what?
> C: Like, is that all it's about? Like we are all just pieces of meat walking around for a while, then that's it?
> T: Those kinds of questions are coming to mind.
> C: You're not supposed to think that stuff. Everybody else seems to be getting on with it but me.

Here is another judgment the client makes about his experience—that people do not, and they are not supposed to, think about the questions he is having about life, death and purpose. Now he is forced to become a philosopher, and he does not like it. This also brings up another aspect of PTG theory. The model of PTG that emphasizes the challenge to, or shattering of, the assumptive world and how survivors struggle with a restructuring of their worldviews or core beliefs. For some, perhaps like the client here, the assumptive world has not even been previously formulated in any clear sense. Some people have their assumptions that they do not question. Others have simply been living life in practical ways without considering their views on major existential issues. The client here has little experience in considering existential issues. Only now is he wondering if we are more than mere bodies, whether we have a dual existence as body and soul, and what is the purpose of our actions during our lives. In his world, people do not consider such questions, and this is creating a sense of alienation. Expert companionship will be important in offsetting this alienation and helping him understand that trauma often opens up the considerations he is having.

T: Others don't find themselves with these thoughts?
C: I don't know—I really don't talk about this stuff. I just try to put it out of my head.
T: I guess it's not working too well so far.
C: So, here I am.
T: Seems like we're doing OK talking about this stuff.

The expert companion is attempting to give the message to the client that his concerns are legitimate, and that discussing them is legitimate, but this client clearly feels that he is in alien territory.

C: Yeah—isn't that what shrinks are supposed to do—listen to people whine about their problems?
T: Think you are whining?
C: No, not really. This stuff is really getting to me. I got to do something. I'm... I don't know... it's like this is just coming back at me all the time.
T: Haunting you.
C: That's it. That's the word... haunting me.
T: I'm glad you decided to come.
C: They pretty much made me.
T: Well, I'm still glad you came.

The ambivalence about needing help continues. The client says he is whining, then recants. He says he has to do something. He says they made him come. The expert companion provides a word for his experience that fits: "haunting." This is important in making a connection to this ambivalent man. And finally, the clinician very explicitly says he is glad the client came. This is the invitation to continue that trauma survivors often need from the expert companion.

In this brief first encounter with this client, the expert companion has begun a certain kind of relationship with the client. This relationship has been characterized by a respectful stance toward the client's experience and toward his worldview, a sincere interest in this experience, a clear invitation to continue, and a recognition of possibilities for PTG. These possibilities include the man's sensitivity, so that he cannot easily put images of what happened and thoughts of Ned and his family, out of his mind. The client also displays his sense of humor that is a bit self-deprecating and does not extend to making fun of what happened to Ned. He has a concern about existential issues that might affect how he chooses to live his own life in the aftermath of this trauma. Even though they may initially be experienced as symptoms or as exclusively negative things by the survivor, all of these can be nurtured into PTG.

Central Components for Working with Growth

Focus on Listening

As we emphasize throughout this book, it is important for the clinician to cultivate the ability to be fully present with the client during all aspects of the therapeutic process. Although it is a bit hyperbolic, what we tell therapists is to *focus on listening without trying to solve*. That is the first step, and it is important throughout the journey that expert companions take with their clients. To work with clients who have experienced trauma and tragedy, clinicians will need a substantial degree of comfort to endure the telling of stories that can sometimes be horrific. Simple listening, without disturbing the telling of the story by the client, and without usurping the affect the clients have in response to their experiences. A clear and quiet presence is probably the most helpful to the client.

There are several empirically supported approaches to treating posttraumatic symptoms, and effective clinicians will introduce them as appropriate for each client (Sharpless & Barber, 2011). However, it is important to resist the temptation to rush in with a perceived solution for the client. The temptation is to provide some expertise, perhaps to give helpful advice, or to provide the psychological equivalent of the written prescription that physicians hand to patients.

The clinician must adopt an attitude of listening to the accounts and narratives that the client develops. It is within those accounts that the experience of posttraumatic growth may become most clearly visible to the therapist. The following quotes provide excellent examples of the kind of stance we are suggesting that clinicians, working with survivors of traumatic events, should take. A pediatric oncologist describes the responses of a young patient to her willingness to simply be still and listen:

> For an agonizing hour he poured out his young-ancient soul. Then he rose from the chair with tears pouring down his face. "You're the best doctor I've ever met," he exclaimed. "No one has ever helped me as much as you have. How can I thank you?" I have never gotten to say a word to Jay. I had only listened. (Komp, 1993, p. 62)

Describing the treatment of posttraumatic stress symptom of veterans, another therapist makes the same point:

The advice that veterans consistently give to trauma therapists is "Listen! Just listen." Respect, embodied in this kind of listening, is readiness to be changed by the narrator. The change may be small or large. It may be simply learning something not previously known, feeling something, seeing something from a new perspective, or it may be as profound as redirection of the listener's way of being in the world. (Shay, 1994, p. 189)

The general suggestion to listen well is part of all types of psychological interventions. Clinicians interested in the possibility of posttraumatic growth in their clients can be more specific.

Notice Growth If the Client Approaches It

The possibility of posttraumatic growth is revealed primarily, but not exclusively, in verbal exchanges. Subsequent chapters will include many examples of such exchanges between therapists and clients. The clinician needs to be prepared to listen for themes of growth and bring them into focus when they are present. It is in the struggle to understand the traumatic circumstances, and then reconcile them with the core beliefs that have been raised or challenged, that growth may be most likely to be seen. The struggle to understand what will happen to one's life, how life can be in the aftermath, and the distress of not believing, or even understanding the tragic new world, can provide the context for the experience of growth. Clinicians need to be attuned to the possibility of growth, and we are suggesting that therapists help the client articulate it if it is present.

Label It If Growth Is There

The clinician may want to explicitly label growth that is only implicit in the client's narrative. To do this effectively and appropriately requires tact and sensitivity. The clinician responds to what may be elements of growth that emerge in the posttraumatic narrative.

For example, a man made an appointment after some weeks of high levels of joint pain that had culminated in the diagnosis of a chronic, recurrently painful, arthritic condition. There was no cure and the condition tended to flare up after long periods of physical activity. Because of that, he was forced to cut back on the physically demanding work that was required on his job, making it necessary for him to accept payments for partial disability. In the first session he said that part of the reason for making the appointment was an interest in marriage counseling because he and his wife had "not gotten along for some time." In a later session, he commented that "over the past couple of weeks" things had gotten better with his wife. He said that his wife was being "real supportive, and I am starting to realize that maybe I have underestimated her," and that he was starting to "appreciate the things she has done for me over the past few months." The clinician responded by indicating that "it sounds like one of the things you are discovering is that, at least in some ways, your condition and your discomfort have served to bring the two of you a little closer together." The therapist's response allowed the client to identify and label a change that has elements of possible posttraumatic growth in an important personal relationship.

But, clinicians must be on guard so they do not offer insensitive platitudes about what wonderful opportunities for growth crises can offer. The goal is to listen carefully and well to the whole story, with all of its components—affective, cognitive, behavioral, and perhaps physical. When clients face circumstances that are still overwhelming, the focus needs to be on helping the client survive and manage basic coping tasks. And after some events, those that involve tragic losses, or events that are repellent and incomprehensible (e.g. the Holocaust), the client may interpret the experience of growth as a sign of disloyalty or a lack of moral principle. In such situations, clinicians must be extremely sensitive about when, or even *if*, to identify or label the possible occurrence of posttraumatic growth. But, when the proper therapeutic relationship is in place, and if the client's own account provides evidence that growth is occurring, it is useful to consider gradually bringing it into focus for the client.

Inquire About the Possibility

Clinicians need to be open about the possibility of growth in their clients, and it may well be that clients will recognize growth before clinicians will. Clinicians should always follow the lead provided by their clients' experiences and their descriptions of those experiences. If the clinician senses the possibility that growth may be emerging or present, but the client has not given explicit indication that such is the case, clinicians can check out the possibility. At the appropriate time on the posttraumatic journey, clinicians might ask something like, "Some people have said that they changed in some positive ways by being forced by life to face very difficult, sometimes traumatic, situations. Do you think that is possible for you, given the kinds of things you went, and are, going through?"

Although many clients are likely to provide evidence of their experience of growth, or they may articulate it in response to a direct search for it, an important reminder (which we will repeat) is in order. Posttraumatic growth, although common, is neither inevitable nor universal.

Choosing the Right Words

When talking with clients about growth, the word choices clinicians make need to reflect that growth comes from the struggle to cope and survive, not from the event itself. Clinicians need to place the semantic focus on the person's *struggle* with what has happened, not with the event itself. It is not the death of a beloved two-year-old that may change a grieving parent, but the parent's long and arduous, and permanently painful struggle to cope that might produce some elements of posttraumatic growth. Clinicians need to be judicious in the way they choose to reflect, label, highlight, or inquire about the possibility of posttraumatic growth.

three
Posttraumatic Growth in Multicultural Context

Kathy had been seriously injured in an automobile wreck. She was on a two-lane state highway, driving from her college to a city about 60 miles away to visit her mother, when the 18-wheeler truck that was coming in the opposite direction crossed the center line and hit her car head on. She was told that the rescue team found her unconscious in the back seat of her older model compact car. Given the seriousness of the accident she was helicoptered from the scene and taken to the university medical center that was only a 15-minute flight away. The skilled staff at the hospital saved her life. She was in a coma for five days, but after waking she began a steady recovery.

When she talked with one our researchers several months later, she was still walking with a slight limp, but otherwise reported that things were going well— and that dealing with the accident had changed her and made her a better person in fundamental ways. She said that she had never felt closer to God, and that it was clear that the previous path she was on was wrong. "I kind of thought of most people as a pain in the ass; they were over there and I was over here. I didn't care about them and lots of the time I found myself angry at them. But now I know that we are all children of God. I need to love them and I need to find out God's plan for my life. I was drifty before, but now I know my life has a purpose. This experience made God real to me."

When clinicians encounter people like this young woman, or the bereaved father we met at the beginning of the first chapter, it is helpful to understand the cultural contexts that influence the client. For example, how can we best respond to a young woman who is seeing a new path for her life, and whose understanding of how she should live her life is heavily influenced by a particular religious tradition? In this chapter we will discuss some of the cultural factors that clinicians generally, and those whose clients seem to be experiencing posttraumatic growth in particular, should try to discover and understand.

In one of our undergraduate classes, students were doing a little exercise to get them started on understanding culture and the cultural factors that influenced them. As the discussion progressed, the instructor asked one of the students if he would like to describe his own cultural background and influences. The student seemed befuddled and then blurted out, "Professor, I don't think I really have any culture or cultural influences—I'm White!" This student amusingly and naïvely did not realize that all human beings are influenced by cultural factors as they develop, and cultural factors continue to play a role in all aspects of their lives. But what is "culture" and which cultural factors may be particularly important and useful for clinicians to understand about their clients? The following discussion focuses on how the expert companion should attend to sociocultural elements with all clients dealing with very difficult situations and, where appropriate, the discussion will focus specifically on posttraumatic growth.

What is Culture?

In early 2012, using the search word culture in the PsychInfo database resulted in a list of 116,358 references. A Boolean search with the terms culture and definition narrowed the list down to a 3,330. These results suggest at least two things. One, the social and behavioral sciences devote much attention to culture. Two, there is no consensus on how culture is to be defined and understood. However, in spite of some disagreements about specifics, there is agreement that understanding cultural influences is important and there is some agreement about the characteristics of "culture."

A key characteristic of culture is that it is socially constructed. Culture is not a direct product of biological factors, but it results from social processes and interactions between people. We may somehow be evolutionary prepared, in a general way, to learn how to work with and behave toward other people, but *what* we do and *how* we interact are brought about by social forces in the environments in which we grow and develop.

Another key characteristic of culture is that it is transmitted, from one generation to the next, by environmental influences. The smaller social units in which we grow up, usually some variation of a family, play key roles in explicitly and implicitly teaching us what we should believe, how we should think, and how we should act. Not only families, but peers also appear to be very important in the process whereby people are enculturated with the elements of the dominant culture of the place they live, and of the many smaller microcultures of which all human beings are a part.

What are some of the components of culture that are transmitted to the next generation, to the new members of a society, or to new members of a smaller socio-cultural unit such as a gang, team, or corporation? The many elements of culture include, but are not limited to, the following: a group's history; the values considered to be important; central beliefs about the world and the group; beliefs about what roles an individual is expected to play and the person's place in the group; rules of conduct for specific social situations; general norms of good or desirable behavior; desirable and undesirable life goals; definitions of success; what it means to live a good life, etc.

Culture, then, can be defined as the set of "ideas, schemas, ... values, norms, goals" (Fiske, 2002, p. 85), rules of conduct, role expectations, social practices, desirable and undesirable life goals, definitions of success, etc. *"that bind members"* (Stuart, 2004, p. 5) of a social group together. Adherence to the beliefs and behaviors of the group's culture tends to be met with social approval, and deviation from those cultural elements tends to be met with some form of social sanction. Thinking of culture in this way indicates that each person can be part of many cultures, ranging from large and heterogeneous groups like "American society," to smaller groupings, such as Lubavitch Hasidism, to an even smaller unit such as a particular Lubavitch community in Brooklyn, NY.

One of our former clients, a very bright and delightful 35-year-old man, illustrates this view that individuals can have many cultural homes. He was gay, his political party affiliation was Republican, he described himself as a "theologically liberal born-again Southern Baptist," and he was considering the possibility of giving up his highly paid corporate job to go to seminary to become a Baptist minister. His list of "cultures" might include the following: being an American; being a Republican; being a man; being part of the broad community of American gay men in general; being part of the local gay community; being a Southern Baptist; being a member of his local church; being a part of his extended family, his partner and their marriage; and if he did indeed go to seminary, the particular culture of the specific seminary where he chose to go.

Why is Culture Important?

A very simple and concrete answer to this question is that professional ethics mandate that clinicians consider their multicultural competence in their clinical work. The American Psychological Association, for example, indicates that psychologists should show a "commitment to cultural awareness and knowledge of self and others" (American Psychological Association, 2003, p. 382). To practice ethically, clinicians of all professions must be sensitive to cultural elements in their work. Good social workers, counselors, pastoral counselors, psychologists, or psychiatrists, then, must have some understanding of cultural elements in their clinical work—our professions mandate it.

The reason that our professions mandate that we commit ourselves to cultural awareness is that cultural elements can contribute to the problems our clients face, cultural elements can influence how clinical work should be done, they can influence which treatment goals are best, and cultural influences can affect the client's well-being when good clinical work produces positive changes for the client that are congruent with the multiple cultures in which our clients live their daily lives.

Broad Categories: Groups and Cultures?

Are ethnicity, gender, and social class cultures? Sometimes they can be and sometimes they are not. The more important question, however, is whether these are the most important cultural elements to consider when working with clients who have experienced a major life crisis, and who may have experienced some version of posttraumatic growth. Membership in subsets of these broad categories may be important, for some clients some of the time, but more specific cultural elements may be more important because they may reflect the specific ways in which these broad cultural affiliations can influence the client. Nevertheless, these broad categories often dominate the discussion about multicultural clinical competence.

They have expanded considerably in recent years, but the ethnic categories that have predominated in the United States, particularly since the administration of President Richard Nixon (Rodriguez, 2002), are as follows: Black (African-American), White (European American or Caucasian), Asian (Asian-American)/ Pacific Islander, Native American/Eskimo (Yupik/Inuit), and Hispanic (Latino). Given American history, particularly slavery and its treatment of African-Americans, and the poor treatment of other ethnic minority groups, it is understandable that many therapists, particularly those who are White, may consciously or unconsciously think of individual clients primarily or exclusively as members of these broad categories. It is important, however, for clinicians to think of cultural factors in ways that are a bit more specific and more complex.

The welcome emphasis on multicultural diversity of recent years may have produced some undesirable consequences that can impact clinical work. One possible unforeseen consequence is that clinicians, by focusing on the client's membership in one of the broad ethnic categories above, may miss the incredible variety of cultures and cultural influences that are present within each of those categories. Hispanic or Latino, for example, can describe persons who are from at least 18 countries on the mainland of the Americas alone. Of those, there about 205,000,000 Brazilians who speak Portuguese, not Spanish. And within that group of Portuguese speakers, considering religion alone, there are adherents of Catholicism, of a variety of Protestant religions, many heavily influenced by Pentecostalism, and of the Afro-Brazilian religions of Candomble´ and Umbanda. And to complicate things further, many Brazilians are distinctly syncretistic in their personal religious views, combining beliefs and elements of more than one of those religions. For example, it is not uncommon for people to attend mass regularly, but also to participate in rituals connected to the Afro-Brazilian religious traditions. As another illustration of how matters can become very complicated within the broad "American" categories for race and ethnicity,

Brazilian Portuguese has up to 127 labels to describe a person's race and skin color (Brazilian Institute of Geography and Statistics, 1999).

Many similar illustrations of the great heterogeneity and complexity of the cultural elements within each of the broad categories of ethnicity commonly used in the United States could be made. Given this wide diversity within the broad categories of race or ethnicity that American clinicians may be using, they must be cautious about their assumptions of what the cultural contexts of, and cultural influences on, individual clients are. Knowing that a particular client is, for example, "Latino" may give the clinician some workable hypothesis about cultural influences, but those workable hypotheses, if not treated with great caution and clinician self-awareness, may reflect damaging stereotypes rather than helpful cultural sensitivities. It is instructive to consider that within one's own culture, there are a variety of proximal influences from community, family and other close relationships that distinguish oneself from other members of the same culture in various ways. So it is with clients, and it is important to avoid generalizations based on culture when doing clinical work.

The history of the United States does include a shameful degree of racism, particularly by European Anglo-Whites towards persons of African, Spanish, and Asian origins. Those historical realities may indeed still influence the daily lives of people who belong to those groups that were historically, and perhaps still are, discriminated against. Clinicians should be aware of those possibilities. However, an approach for working with individuals, couples, or families, that is applicable to every clinical case, is to approach clients as unique, and to relate to them and understand them within that uniqueness, particularly their cultural uniqueness. The "Latino" persons that become your clients may fit at least in some ways, within the broad confines of what you believe, or have been taught, about Latin culture. And yes, it may be possible, in the very broadest terms, to identify general cultural differences between large groups of people, for example, the more collectivist culture of Japan and the more individualistic culture of North America (Fiske, 2002; Nisbett, 2003). However, viewing clients only within the limited window of their membership in broad cultural categories, categories that in many ways are themselves specific products of a specific geographic, cultural, and historical periods, is likely to lead clinicians into the trap of seeing clients primarily as members of a very broad category, rather than as individual human beings.

With these general admonitions about putting a client only into one of a few categories of ethnicity or race, categories probably created for political reasons in the United States (Rodriguez, 2002), is there some utility in thinking about ethnicity, gender, and class as comprising useful cultural categories? As one psychologist suggests, "not every group has, or makes up, a culture" (Cohen, 2010, p. 59). Just because an individual belongs to a particular group does not mean that the group constitutes a culture, and that is an important reminder.

But is it possible that growing up as a member of one or the other gender, or of a particular ethnic group, or of a particular social class, will have a significant cultural influence on an individual client? Certainly that is the case, and any clinician who has worked, for example, with male clients who are reluctant to self-disclose and discuss their inner psychological states has encountered the effects of North American male "culture" (Shay, 1996). African-Americans in the United States are more likely than Whites to have experienced discrimination and this commonality of experience may create some degree of shared beliefs that may reflect common bonds that can be regarded as a shared culture (Corning & Buchianneri, 2010). In a similar vein, the experience of people who grow up in the lower social class may lead them to have some similarities, for example, a greater degree of empathic accuracy than people raised in the upper socio-economic class (Kraus, Piff, & Keltner, 2011).

One's gender, ethnicity, social class, or other sets of similar restricted cultural categories for classifying people, may indeed constitute a culture, and multicultural awareness of how memberships in these broad categories may also reflect broad cultural differences is important (Weiss & Berger, 2010). But the obvious admonition is that although awareness of the possible impact of such factors and of the historical elements that have influenced members of those groups is important, knowing the client's category does not reliably tell the clinician anything specific about individual people, about the tragedies they have encountered, or how unique cultural niches may or may not influence the possibility and the process of their experience of posttraumatic growth. There are, however, a number of specific cultural elements that affect people, and that are useful and important for clinicians to learn about and understand about people.

Social and Multicultural Elements in Posttraumatic Growth

Primary Reference Groups

All of us belong to groups of people with whom we interact. The social group may be formally organized, for example, a sports team, legally recognized, for example, a married couple with children, or informally organized, for example a group of friends in a neighborhood or a gang of adolescent boys. Of all of the groups to which clients belong, the groups that have significant social influence on them are called *primary reference groups*. A key question in ascertaining a client's primary reference groups is "Which groups does the individual want to please, whose opinions does the client value, and whose approval does the client seek?" More colloquially, which groups does the client identify with?

Although there are exceptions, most people want the approval and acceptance of their families, of their group of friends, members of their clubs, the local religious group of which they are members, and so on. Connected to the previous discussion of broad groups, some persons may see the rather broad ethnic category to which they belong as a primary reference group. Although not universal, persons who belong to demographic groups that are minorities, or who lack significant social and political power, may also see themselves as belonging to the broader, more abstract group that constitutes a particular ethnic group, social class, or religion.

It is important for the clinician to listen for clues for the persons and groups that are important to clients, and for clues about the degree to which those have social influence on clients. Depending on the kind of crisis that the person is struggling with, that person may see him or herself as a member of the group of people who have experienced similar tragedies. Soldiers wounded in combat may see themselves as part of the community of wounded veterans and bereaved parents may see themselves as fellow citizens of the same "country." Other persons who have faced similar tragedies may have a higher degree of credibility, so that the person in crisis will value their support and guidance more than that offered by somebody who is not a citizen of the same "country."

Some years ago one of our students did a very small and exploratory study on the social support experienced by persons who had lost a close family member to suicide (Wagner & Calhoun, 1991). She talked to bereaved family members and to people in their social networks, people who had tried to provide support in the aftermath of the loss. She found something interesting. The bereaved family tended to divide the people in their broader social networks into two categories: people who had, and people who had not, experienced a similar loss. Although it is a tentative conclusion, the findings suggested that both groups of people engaged in pretty much the same kinds of supportive actions, with the same frequency. However, the surviving family members *experienced* the supportive gestures of similarly bereaved people as more helpful. There is clearly more than the simple impact of a primary reference group at work, but this small study provides an interesting lesson. There will be some people in the client's social worlds who will have significant influence over them, including how they experience the traumatic event—and clinicians should try to learn who those people are.

Primary reference groups are also important because they are the most likely sources of effective social support for persons in highly stressful situations. Which groups can provide useful services, material assistance if needed, emotional support, and helpful information to the client? When people experience a loss or other crisis, social groups can be a powerful source of comfort. Wise counselors not only try to learn who those groups may be, but also do their best to ascertain which groups are most likely to be effective in the provision of the kinds of support that people need.

As the model of growth described in Chapter 1 indicates, sociocultural influences may also influence the likelihood and the process of posttraumatic growth. An important set of cultural influences on growth are the individual's primary reference groups. The model suggests that one important way in which the process of growth can be influenced by primary reference groups is through the availability of models of growth. The evidence suggests that is exactly the case. In samples of people who experienced domestic violence, and people who had been diagnosed with cancer, those who said that they knew somebody else who had experienced posttraumatic growth reported higher levels of growth than people who did not know such a person (Cobb, Tedeschi, Calhoun, & Cann, 2006; Weiss, 2004).

The model also suggests that responses to self-disclosure of elements of posttraumatic growth, to members of primary reference groups, may play a role in the process, and perhaps the likelihood, of growth. It is not, however, the simple fact of self-disclosure that is likely to be important, but the combination of such self-disclosure, with accepting and supportive responses to the disclosure by members of primary reference groups.

Finding out as much as possible about the individual's primary reference groups is an important part of culturally sensitive clinical work. It is also important because primary reference groups can influence the experience of posttraumatic growth.

Social Rules and Norms

These two terms, social rules and social norms mean the same general thing. They describe expectations about what people can do, should do, or should not do. In general, rules tend to describe the norms for very specific social situations, for example, what is expected of people at a funeral. Norms tend to apply more broadly, for example, how boys and girls are expected to dress. Regardless of technical distinctions in meaning, these words describe the expectations, perhaps even rigid "laws," that are held in common by members of particular groups. Following the group's rules gains acceptance and perhaps praise, and violation of the rules can result in social sanctions, expulsion from the group, or worse.

Therapists need to learn as much as they can about the social norms and social rules of the primary reference groups that have influence on the client. The norms that are most relevant will vary with circumstance, but for work with trauma survivors, with a focus on the possibility of growth, the rules about self-disclosure can play an important role. There are likely to be expectations about the expression of emotions in general, and there may also be a separate set of social expectations for member of particular groups. For example, among some cultural groups it is expected that women will, or at least are allowed, to cry freely and openly about the life crisis they are experiencing, but men are often expected to exhibit a greater degree of control over the expression of their emotions. It is still the case that, in many parts of North America, some expression of emotion by people facing personal tragedies is tolerated and even anticipated; however, adults are generally expected to express their emotions with some degree of decorum. One person has articulated this general social rule like this: "I think they [survivors] should try to control their emotions... It could be a more proper way... Try to keep themselves under control" (Perry, 1993, p. 58).

Trauma survivors who are part of some sociocultural groups may experience this need to appear in emotional control, much as the person just quoted would want them to be. Members of other social groups, however, such as in some

Mexican communities, may feel free to engage in the expression of emotions in ways that are "perhaps more open and demonstrative" than in many Anglo communities (Younoszai, 1993, p. 77).

People dealing with major life crises may also suffer because most laypersons, and perhaps clinical professionals too, do not know what they should or can do to provide support, because of the lack of clarity of the social rules for the provision of support and comfort for people in crisis. People who might be sources of social support may feel constrained by that lack of clarity and may choose to do nothing, rather than run the risk of engaging in interactions where they may feel or be perceived as socially inadequate or socially insensitive (Calhoun, Abernathy, & Selby, 1984, 1986). This potential discomfort on the part of members of the person's primary reference groups may somehow get communicated to the persons in crisis, making their already challenging situations even more socially awkward and stressful for them. The social discomfort of potential caregivers can lead persons dealing with traumatic events to feel even more disconnected from the very people who might otherwise be perceived as sources of help and support.

It is not only the rules about self-disclosure generally that are important, but also those that may exist about the disclosure of themes of posttraumatic growth. The available evidence suggests that in North America, themes of posttraumatic growth are generally plentiful in the wider society (McAdams, 2006; Lindstrom, et al., 2011). In some contexts, however, talking to others about those themes may be regarded as too boastful or arrogant. In Japan, for example, revealing to others the greater sense of personal strength and resilience, that some people feel as a result of their struggle with major difficulties, tends to be regarded as impolite; speaking to others about one's individual positive change tends to be viewed as inappropriate.

The kind of response that people receive when they do articulate their experience of growth may also play a role in the process. Our guiding assumption is that when self-disclosures about posttraumatic growth are met with social acceptance or support, they are more likely to lead to a clearer sense that growth has indeed occurred. Overall, social groups that support the kind of self-disclosure about their situation that trauma survivors want to make, and that support appropriate disclosures about growth themes, are more likely to encourage not only effective coping, but posttraumatic growth as well.

What the Good Life Is

Many persons who experience posttraumatic growth change their understanding of what the good life is. This change is reflected in altered priorities, greater appreciation for life, and changes in the existential, spiritual, or religious dimensions of life. Although for the person such changes are regarded as highly desirable, and perhaps as life changing, the revised life narrative and modified priorities may clash with the norms for judging what the good life is held by the individual's primary reference groups.

Krystie J. was a 40-year-old, very successful, director of athletics at a prestigious college. She had been at the same school for several years, and had been promoted up the ranks from assistant coach of the lacrosse team to director of all sports. She had been an athletic, energetic, and healthy woman all her life. The diagnosis of pancreatic cancer was not only shocking, but devastating. She sought help from a psychotherapist early in the medical process and continued the relationship through treatment and eventually to the welcome news that the disease was in remission.

After a long process of careful deliberation, she decided that she was making a radical shift in what she would do with the rest of her life. She had always considered doing something that directly benefited marginalized poor people, but had never done anything specific. She decided that now she would, and obtained a position with a small nonprofit group that focused on providing nutritional school lunches for children in public schools deep in rural Appalachia. Her salary would be less than half of what she was making and she would be living in a small town, far from any urban center. From her perspective, she was finally answering a call she had felt, to make a difference with her life. For her nuclear and extended families, however, her decision was not only puzzling, but viewed, as one of her uncles put it, "totally nuts!"

For her family, the prevailing measure of a good and successful life was achieving a combination of wealth and high social status. Her job as athletic director had given her some degree of social prominence. But her decision to work for a nonprofit, at a lower salary, "out in hillbilly country," removed the only marker of living life well that her family believed she had. Her decision dramatically violated the norms her family had about how life should be lived. She initially received no support from them, and one or two directly told her the decision was crazy, but eventually her sister and both her parents developed some degree of acceptance of, and support for, what she had decided to do.

Krystie's situation also demonstrates how posttraumatic growth can represent a threat to core beliefs that are culturally based, and can put trauma survivors in the difficult position of challenging aspects of their own cultures, perhaps putting them at odds with others in their primary references groups. Clinicians must understand the core beliefs that have been previously held as well as the new, emerging set of beliefs. The expert companion accompanies trauma survivors as they sort through the internal and the interpersonal conflicts that may occur. Here is an example of how this can be done.

Robert was a 22-year-old man who was adopted as an infant from Mexico by Caucasian parents in Chicago. He grew up in an upper middle class suburb as an only child. He did well in school, felt loved by his parents, but always had a sense that his skin color was an obstacle in his social relationships, although he rarely encountered overt racism. He had recently graduated from college when he suffered a brain injury in a motorcycle accident and spent several months in a rehabilitation center. There he met some young Latino men who were also undergoing rehabilitation. These men were from poor neighborhoods and had suffered injuries during gang fights. Robert found them to be rough, religious, and surprisingly kind and accepting of him, despite their socio-economic differences. Here is an excerpt from a session that took place mid-way through his rehabilitation.

R: You know, these guys call me Roberto. I like it, I feel like one of them. It suits me.

T: Even though you have always been Robert.

R: Yeah, it's weird—I feel more like Roberto than Robert.

T: A connection there.

R: I told my folks about this and they got really worried. My mom said "You'd better watch out with those guys. You don't want them bothering you when they get out of there."

T: Like they are dangerous.

R: Yeah. I realize they could be I guess—or people they know. It's obvious enough—they got shot. I just tell her not to worry. Dad, too. He wants me to keep my distance. He says it's fine to be supportive to them, but just don't invite them home.

T: I get the feeling you are unsure this is right.

R: These guys are being good to me, so I shouldn't think of them as dangers to me. I don't want to be a hypocrite and be nice to them in the hospital and then be thinking I've got to be sure to get away from them. But I am a little wary, I mean I wouldn't want to hang out with them in their place—I think that would be dangerous. So I'm not going to do that, but I just feel a certain comfort around them. You know, my Spanish is getting better—that's pretty cool.

In this exchange, Robert is engaging in a reconsideration of his parents' stance on relationships with people outside their social class, and he is developing a sense of connectedness with people who grew up very differently from him, but with whom he has a common heritage. In a session a few weeks later, Robert reports the following.

R: It is so weird; these guys are very religious, even though they are in a gang. Hector was telling me that he saw me talking to my Mom and I should be more respectful to my mother. It is so strange, I can't figure these guys out. I just think that they should be bad guys but they really aren't.

T: They don't fit with the expectations you've had.

R: I never met anyone like them before, I guess I was just going on what I see on TV and what I was brought up with. Last week I went over to see my aunt and uncle and we were talking politics because of the election, and Uncle Fred was getting into it about illegal immigrants and I just found myself getting really defensive. Uncle Fred says he's such a good Christian and can talk so hatefully, and I'm thinking "Hector and Julio are better than you Uncle Fred—you'd be surprised."

T: He would be surprised if you said that.

R: Oh man, I'd never say that to Uncle Fred. He's always been good to me. It's getting pretty confusing, you know? Like, am I this upper middle class college graduate, or maybe I'm this Mexican guy—you know some people see me that way—I've always had a bit of that to deal with. But I always tried to get away from that. But Hector and Julio, they are real people. Julio's mom came to the hospital and I met her. She can't speak English so I had to use my Spanish, but she was as sweet as can be, and she told me that Julio said I was helping him and how grateful she was for that, and she started to cry. These people are so real, you know? I feel like I could be part of them. I look like them. I'm speaking Spanish.

T: Like you are knowing part of yourself you have never known before.

R: Exactly.

T: I guess this is a good thing?

R: Feels good, a bit scary, confusing.

T: I guess it makes you look at other people, and yourself, differently.

R: Makes me look at guys like Hector and Julio different than I would have looked at them before, and my family a little different, too. I don't like some of the things I see in them. I hate to say this, but there is some racism there. I mean, I've always been treated as one of the family, even though I have brown skin. But they treat other people who look just like me as threats, and they don't even know them.

T: Getting to know them makes a difference.

R: If I hadn't been in this hospital with them, I never would have known, either.

T: So you know stuff you didn't know before.

R: I think I've got stuff to learn from Hector and Julio I never would have thought about before. I guess I wish I could be a little more like them, and maybe they could be a little more like me. Not get mixed up with all the crazy gang stuff.

T: Have you said that to them?

R: Yeah, they just say that's the way it is—a real fatalistic attitude. That I don't care for, but I guess it is understandable where they come from.

T: So what part of them would you like to be more like?

R: I guess the warmth, acceptance I see in them and their families. The emotion there. I know that has to sound strange that I'd say these gang guys are warm, and emotional. I don't say it to my family—they'd think I was nuts. But you know what I'm saying?

T: I think I do. These guys are very direct with you and accept you without any apparent conditions.

R: Right, they're straight up.

T: No hidden agendas.

R: I really don't think so. It's funny. You would think gang members would be very wary.

T: Maybe they are in the street, but not so much in the hospital.

R: Yeah, maybe so.

T: You haven't seen them on the street.

R: Yeah, that might be different.

T: There may be different sides to them.

R: Got to be, I guess.

T: Maybe there are different sides to you, too.

R: I think that's what's happening. I'm seeing a different side.

T: You grew up in one culture, but are also attracted to another.

R: Right. I can't figure out—maybe it's because of my skin, my looks, I can identify. If I really was just a white guy, maybe I wouldn't.

T: Or maybe Hector and Julio wouldn't have approached you as readily.

R: That could be.

T: But they are giving you an opportunity to learn something about yourself, or maybe how you want to live, what you want to believe.

R: Who I am.

T: Right.

R: This accident set the stage for the whole thing, but if they hadn't been here at the same time, I wonder. I guess it was both the accident and them.

T: Also, maybe your willingness to be open to them, rather than be as wary as your family told you to be.

R: I wonder where this is all going to take me. It worries me, because I see things in my family I don't like so much. And I am really not sure about keeping up with Hector and Julio. How would that work? But you know, there is something I am feeling pretty sure about.

T: What's that?

R: I need to get more involved with Mexican culture—I feel like it is mine somehow, even though I never lived it, I was adopted out of it.

T: Who knows how these things work—the sense of roots and belonging.

R: My life is getting more complicated but also I think it could be richer.

T: So, are you Robert or Roberto?

R: Hah! You know I've been going by Roberto with Hector and Julio. But I can't be Roberto with my family. I guess both, for now.

For Robert, cultural issues became the direct focus of posttraumatic growth. Cultural perspectives are important components of the assumptive world. For Robert, the struggle with the traumatic event itself—the motorcycle accident—was not what was producing change. Instead, the accident placed Robert in new circumstances that challenged his beliefs, and exposed him to support from people who introduced new ways of looking at life. We could also say that Robert might have been primed for this change, given he was adopted and might have always had some interest in his birth culture, and that he was 22 years old and perhaps open to consideration of life change.

We can also imagine that in the sessions with Robert, the clinician needed to learn about the social norms and beliefs characteristic of *all* of Robert's various cultures, so that as an expert companion, he could accompany Robert on the exploration of change in core beliefs, identity, and ways of relating to others. To be most effective, clinicians working with persons who face difficult situations need to know much about the social rules and norms that guide the behavior of their clients, and the behavior of those persons in their important social groups. Such knowledge is not only important for clinical work generally, but also for working with clients for whom the experience of posttraumatic growth is possible.

Assumptions About What Helps

What assumptions do you make about the curative ingredients of psychological interventions? Most clinicians can readily articulate their ideas about what those curative elements are. Cognitively focused therapies assume that helping clients change their thought patterns to more adaptive ways will lead to a reduction in psychological distress. The assumption on which cognitive therapy is based, for example, is that how people think directly affects how they feel; changing habitual thoughts to more adaptive ways of thinking is expected lead to a reduction in psychological distress. There is also very good empirical evidence that certain qualities of the therapeutic relationship, for example, accurate empathy expressed by the therapist and a strong therapeutic alliance produce better therapeutic outcomes (Norcross & Wampold, 2011).

The assumptions that clients, or the people who influence them, make about what helps, may sometimes be quite different from those that highly trained therapists make. Although it may occur less often now than it did some years ago, it is still common to have potential clients ask "how will talking about this make any difference, because it won't solve my problem." A client from rural Appalachia, for example, firmly believed that his serious depression was caused by "bad nerves" and only some kind of "nerve medicine" would help; just talking about things certainly would not.

Attending to the cultural ways of understanding about what can help people who are in the midst of life crises, particularly when that understanding differs from the clinician's, is important. Failure to acknowledge and understand those differing points of view may impair the clinician's ability to develop the most helpful therapeutic relationship.

The Clinician's Social Status and Social Role

> Doctor, you are an expert on stress. I am currently very stressed by my job. Tell me what I should do so that I will deal effectively and overcome my stress.

This was a request from an executive from a country in Asia where "doctors" are expected to utilize their expertise to offer an expert solution to a patient. The "doctor" is expected to make a diagnosis of the problem and then to prescribe a solution. For this client, and within the cultural groups to which he belonged, psychologists were seen as having reasonably high status, and the role of the "doctor" was seen as that of a wise and knowledgeable person who could offer a solution to specific problems. In this instance, the clinician did not resist the role into which the client had cast him, but worked within that role to provide the best help possible. The clinician's style of expert companionship may need to differ, at least somewhat, for clients embedded in different cultural contexts.

Because there are variations between cultural groups regarding their appropriate roles and their social status, clinicians should develop an awareness of how they are viewed by their clients, and how mental health professionals are viewed by members of the client's primary reference groups. In contrast to the high status accorded to the psychologist by the client described above, many practicing clinicians have experience with clients who indicate that people they know assume that psychological interventions are ineffective and a waste of time. Some clients, who belong to some Christian religious groups, may regard mental health professionals with some caution, because clinicians are assumed to be agnostics or atheists, and consequently are assumed to have some disdain for traditional religious beliefs. These kinds of assumptions, about who clinicians are, may lead some members of the client's social groups to actively discourage people they know from seeking professional help from persons outside of the religious group, or to encourage them to discontinue treatment if already begun.

Sociocultural Consequences of Change

To the extent that psychological interventions produce good results, those results usually involve some kind of change on the part of the client. Although the desired ends of intervention may differ between client and counselor at the beginning of the counseling relationship, greater congruence of goals is likely to occur over time. Another important cultural aspect to consider, then, is how therapeutic changes will be perceived in the client's social world. How will the primary social groups respond to the changes the client undergoes? For example, how will others respond to a man whose growth is reflected in greater freedom in self-disclosure and in the honest expression of emotion (Shay, 1996)? We might well imagine that this new skill will be highly appreciated by some of his important others, but in some of his cultural contexts—for example, with male friends who are also reluctant to engage in self disclosure—ready expression of intimate feelings may result in awkwardness, and perhaps significant social sanctions or, worse still, public ridicule. Although a therapeutic process that encourages the expression of inner states and painful feelings may be a good choice, even for a highly reluctant man, the clinician should try to obtain the best understanding possible of what may happen if the man does indeed practice his new-found skills outside of the therapeutic context.

Similar kinds of considerations must be made regarding all aspects of the client's experience of posttraumatic growth. As noted previously, the appropriateness of talking about certain kinds of growth, for example, a greater sense of personal strength and resilience, varies across cultural contexts and, in some, such disclosures may be considered impolite or arrogant (Weiss & Berger, 2010). Therapists need to be aware of the possible responses that the client's differing cultural groups may have not only to broad therapeutic changes that can come about as the result of helpful interventions for traumatic distress, but also to the more specific changes that clients experience as posttraumatic growth. Knowledge about the cultural factors that may have played a role in leading the client to experience growth, and the cultural factors that may encourage or constrain the experience itself or the disclosure of the experience are important considerations when working with any person.

Semantics of Growth

The phrase "posttraumatic growth" has only been around for about 18 years (Tedeschi & Calhoun, 1995) and most laypersons have never heard it. When we use it, people sometimes assume that we are talking about some form of positive thinking and having a positive attitude about their situation. It is possible that this is a general cultural cognitive set for North Americans, so it may be wise for therapists to be cautious about using that specific term. Because of the potential for misunderstanding, it may not always be a good idea to use that term with clients.

The five factors of the Posttraumatic Growth Inventory suggest some of the typical domains in which people report the positive changes that can come from the struggle with traumatic events. Those factors can give clinicians a guide for the kinds of themes to attend to when trying to discern if clients have experienced growth in some form, and the five factors can also suggest some of the kinds of words to use when exploring the possibilities of growth. Speaking of changes in oneself, one's priorities, greater appreciation, relationships with others, and in spiritual or existential matters require no use of the phrase posttraumatic growth or of its many scholarly synonyms.

This is not a recommendation never to use the term posttraumatic growth, but only to be cautious about it. There will be clients who find the term very helpful, since it provides a name for changes they have experienced, but for which they have had no name. In general, however, clinicians can listen for, notice, and perhaps even inquire about posttraumatic growth in their clients, without ever having to use that particular terminology.

A Final Word

Although attending to the broad categories into which most human beings fit, including nationality, ethnicity, and gender, can provide some clinicians with some general working hypotheses about the typical experience of groups of people, that kind of general knowledge is insufficient. Expert companions need to learn as much as they can about the individual niches their clients occupy. They need to understand the various different cultures that influence the client and the varied beliefs, assumptions, and experiences that have shaped that person, and that will continue to exert significant influence on that person, particularly in the domain of posttraumatic growth.

four
Understanding Trauma Response as a Precursor to Growth

An important step in trauma treatment is helping clients understand that the physical and emotional responses they experienced during the traumatic event and afterwards are part of the normal human reaction to threatening circumstances. A short introduction to the basics of the sympathetic nervous system response, often known to clients as the fight-flight-freeze response can be quite reassuring (Phoenix, 2007). The process of labeling and describing the responses clients have experienced provides a sense that they are understood, their experiences are valid, and they are not so different from others. This psychoeducation is part of the early sessions of therapy, but will be referred to throughout treatment. But beyond these basics about the immediate response to a traumatic event, there must be some understanding of how the symptoms of traumatic stress or PTSD grow out of the initial experience. It is not necessary to get technical about this, and often metaphors are useful in the explanations.

Since we are focused here on facilitating PTG, we also help trauma survivors understand that there are other effects of being traumatized that can set the stage for PTG. These effects have to do with the challenge to the trauma survivor's worldview, or core belief system. This is another aspect of the distress that accompanies trauma, but the one that we will emphasize because it is most clearly linked with the development of PTG. What the therapist must be able to do is to explain the PTG model in a simplified fashion that shows how the experience of the aftermath of trauma is understandable, and can eventually lead to PTG.

Here is an early session of trauma treatment that incorporates the psychoeducation about sympathetic nervous system response and the challenge to the core belief system with a view toward PTG. This client was fishing with his friend in the middle of a lake, when his friend appeared to have a seizure, fell overboard and drowned.

C: This is the most upsetting thing I have ever been through. And I am not saying upsetting to mean that it is just a small problem. I mean upsetting everything. Suddenly I am not even myself anymore. I can't believe I couldn't handle it and now I can't handle anything it seems.
T: Not yourself?
C: I'm just a mess. I can't think of anything else it seems. I'm full of anxiety. I can't sleep. I just keep seeing Jeff's face going under. It's horrifying. I get all panicky again.
T: William, I know this is all mystifying and horrifying, but I have to tell you that it is understandable. You didn't really have a chance to prepare for this so it's not surprising it has created trouble for you.

This is a client who is having trouble articulating how the drowning of his friend has affected him. The first statement by the therapist is the beginning of psychoeducation, but it could be hard for a client to listen to this. So it is necessary to be an expert companion and make sure that the client knows that the therapist really understands the depth of the experience.

C: But I always thought of myself as capable. I've learned I'm not, when the chips are down.
T: It's hard to tell what you will actually do in a situation like this. Of course you hope you will be at your best.
C: I never thought I'd be in a situation like that. It was just surreal.
T: I know you told me that you prided yourself on being strong, responsible…
C: And I failed miserably at the most important moment. I just panicked.
T: You told me that it all took you by surprise and you had trouble thinking. I know you feel terrible about this.
C: I could have saved him if I wasn't so freaked out.
T: I remember you said the seizure was the first thing that freaked you out.
C: Yeah, and then everything happened so fast. I didn't know what to do, and before I knew it he slipped into the water.
T: I get the feeling that it will be hard to ever feel OK about this.
C: How could I ever feel OK? Jeff's dead, and I was the only one who could have saved him.
T: That's why you're here, isn't it, because you can't figure out how to ever be OK again.

The therapist tries here to remind the trauma survivor that he hopes that this misery isn't all there is going to be for him, and that he came to therapy looking for some hope.

C: I guess I want to know if this is just going to be my life. I don't know how to do it differently, to feel OK. I would like it to be OK, but it doesn't even seem right to feel OK. I don't have the right. But I hate the idea of just feeling horrible and guilty the rest of my life. I don't know what's OK. And I can't stop thinking about it all.

This is the ambivalence of many trauma survivors about their recovery. If someone has died, bereaved persons often feel that any kind of positive experience is a betrayal of the person who has died. Of course, in "survivor guilt," the very fact that one is a survivor seems like a betrayal of one who has died. The clinician will need to address these reactions that are commonplace to those who experience these traumatic losses without losing the idiosyncratic aspects of the client's experience.

T: Would it help if I explained to you a little about your reactions on the lake, and what you have been going through since?
C: I guess. It is just a confusing mess—I just can't stop thinking about it.
T: Well, of course no explanation of what has happened to you is going to make everything OK, but I'm hoping that you won't be quite as guilty and disappointed with yourself.
C: I'm more than disappointed—disgusted—that's not even it—completely, I don't know, I just feel terrible, that I couldn't save Jeff.
T: That you feel so terrible about it shows how you had higher expectations for yourself, and how much you cared for Jeff.
C: Why couldn't have I just kept my head—maybe I could have found him.
T: Let's talk about that part.
C: How I panicked?
T: Yes. Do you remember how the whole thing started?

The clinician can act as an expert companion by getting the details of the trauma and therefore will be able to understand the experience not just objectively but subjectively. At the same time, discussing the event is part of standard trauma therapy practice in exposure therapy. But not all trauma survivors are as ready as this one to describe their experiences.

In this session, the client William spends some time describing in detail the moment when he realized Jeff, who was sitting behind him in the boat, was having a seizure, how he panicked and moved too quickly, tipping the small boat, and Jeff fell into the water.

C: It all happened so quickly.
T: So quickly that you had no chance to get your thoughts together.
C: I jumped in after him, but I had no idea where he was, and the lake was kind of murky—and it was still so early—I just couldn't see anything. And I was so panicked, I couldn't breathe. Finally I got back in the boat, took some

breaths and jumped in again. But it was too late. I couldn't think of anything to do.

T: I can only imagine how you must have felt.

C: Helpless, scared. I sat there and cried. I got back to shore and called 911. And then I just sat there in the silence. Until I heard the sirens, and then they all started showing up. I just sat there—I couldn't look. They put a blanket over me. They were asking what happened, where we were. But of course it was hopeless. You see, if I had just been calm, the boat wouldn't have tipped, and Jeff probably wouldn't have fallen in. He'd be alive.

T: This is terrible to live with.

The expert companion takes time to continue to attempt to understand the experience of the trauma survivor, even though he or she is in the midst of working on helping the client understand trauma response. Being an expert companion does not mean eschewing expertise, but weaving it into a clear empathic understanding of the clients' experience and their pace in working through their reactions to trauma.

C: I just don't know how to live with it. See, it was all my fault. If had just not panicked!

T: Do you know this panic is actually part of the normal reactions people have to threat, and life and death situations. Have you heard of the fight or flight response?

C: Yes.

T: Do you know what that is?

C: When people get ready to run or fight to protect themselves.

T: Right—it produces changes in the brain and body to do that.

C: But I wasn't trying to protect myself—I was just trying to get to Jeff.

T: But it was immediately clear to you that it was some kind of emergency, and you reacted with all that energy that people have when their brain has quickly turned on this fight or flight response.

C: Adrenaline.

T: Right. Your heart rate shoots up, your blood pressure, too, your breathing gets rapid...

C: Yeah, exactly—that's how I felt.

T: Right—and you leaped into action.

C: I wish I hadn't done it like that.

T: You were primed by your brain and body.

C: And I didn't stop to think.

T: Right. This is just an automatic emergency reaction.

The clinician works in a collaborative way with the client to incorporate the expert knowledge of the expert companion with the specific experience of the client. It is not necessary to get into technical details, however. There is just enough discussion of the sympathetic nervous system response to accomplish the task of addressing the self-blame of the trauma survivor.

> C: Other people in emergencies don't do this.

Here the client insists on his failure. It takes a while to shift the perspective of a trauma survivor who has been engaging in self-blame. Notice that in this case, understanding trauma response may be crucial to self-forgiveness. William has labeled his reaction as "panic," which the clinician is beginning to challenge as he teaches about the sympathetic nervous system response.

> T: Yes, they do. The difference in your case is that it all went bad so quickly, you had no time to get your wits about you. It seems that within a couple of seconds Jeff was in the water.
> C: Yeah, I moved so quickly, the boat began to rock and he was already slumped over the side with the seizure going on. And suddenly, he was gone.
> T: I think there are a couple of things to remind yourself about this. First, other people may not react in panic because they have been trained. Do you remember the firefighters and police who showed up?
> C: Sort of—I was trying not to look at too much, I was just so upset.
> T: These people had been trained to handle these situations, so they had specific roles to play, and performed them. Do you remember?
> C: Yeah.
> T: They had to train to get that way.
> C: Yeah, I sure wasn't.
> T: No, you weren't.
> C: I know CPR.
> T: You might have done CPR.
> C: But I couldn't find him.
> T: If you had, do you think you would have done CPR?
> C: Yeah, I would have tried.
> T: You were trained in this?
> C: I had a course, but I never really had to do it before.
> T: Too bad you didn't get a chance to do this for Jeff. You might have been able to save him if you found him.
> C: Yeah, I wish I had.
> T: Of course.
> C: I really do.
> T: I know—there is no doubt about that.

These simple remarks are a way to cement the therapeutic alliance and at the same time further a mutual perspective that the client did all he could under terrible circumstances.

C: I tried.

T: The circumstances were all wrong.

C: It was kind of dark—it was impossible to see in that water.

T: And you were taken completely off guard, and Jeff was hanging over the side of the boat.

C: It was all a mess.

T: There is another thing to remember about this. Do you realize how different all this would have been if Jeff had had that seizure when you were on land?

The clinician has been a companion who has thoroughly understood this trauma survivor's perspective by taking in the details of the story. This expert companionship allows the clinician to earn the right to challenge his perspective.

C: I guess.

T: Well, think. You still would have been taken by surprise, but if he had fallen on land, it might have been a situation where the seizure comes to an end and Jeff is OK.

C: Even if I had panicked, it wouldn't have been so bad.

T: Exactly. And remember, the "panic" you describe is a reaction of the sympathetic nervous system arousal—the fight or flight response. I think you were just reacting—getting into action—in a situation you had almost no time to appraise before the boat tipped and all went wrong. On land you would have had time to make an appraisal of the situation, and perhaps respond in a way that was perfectly appropriate.

The clinician here makes explicit the relabeling of the "panic" as a normal response to an emergency, and the circumstances playing a major role.

C: I wish it had been that way.

T: But I hope that you can see this has more to do with the circumstances than your capability—and culpability.

C: I guess.

T: First, you had no training or preparation for such an improbable situation. Second, your automatic, and I would say natural response to the emergency was action—just what the fight or flight response is about. And because things went wrong so quickly you did not have time to modulate this response, before a greater emergency was confronting you with Jeff under water. And the fact this happened on the water made it so much more dangerous and difficult to respond to.

The clinician reiterates the perspective that relieves the trauma survivor of blame, and it appears to begin to make an impact.

C: I still wish it hadn't happened.

T: Of course—people always think about how it could be different. This is normal, too. But that can be different from blaming yourself. Do you think my explanation is factual and accurate?

The clinician is using some standard CBT techniques here, focusing on facts and accuracy to bolster a perspective that allows for more constructive responses (Barlow, 2008; Yadin & Foa, 2007). The other thing that is happening here is the client reporting part of his rumination—counterfactual thinking. The clinician does not focus on this except for one statement indicating that this is a common reaction. This could be expanded upon, i.e., the differences between counter-factual thinking and self-blame (Mandel & Dhami 2005). But the focus at this point is on the issue of how to relabel the panic.

C: I guess I can't really argue with it. So the panic was kind of the adrenaline getting to me?

Here the client is beginning to understand very clearly how the normal trauma response was what was occurring in him when Jeff had the seizure, not "panic." This has great implications for how the trauma survivor proceeds from here. Without this, PTG would likely be very difficult. To find something of value coming out of the experience that he sees as his fault might be another betrayal of his friend.

T: Yes, and remember, on land this would not have been a problem.
C: But in that little boat out there, it was.
T: It was under those particular circumstances.
C: It was about the circumstances, you're saying.
T: I'm not just saying—these are the facts you told me. I added in what I know about how the sympathetic nervous system response. That's the truth of it.

Again, the clinician is using CBT techniques to emphasize that he is not just putting a positive spin on the story. He is referring to the details told by the client and information about the sympathetic nervous system response.

C: Jeff was a victim of circumstances.
T: And you, too.

So far, we have been examining in this example the way attention to response to the traumatic event can inhibit recovery and create unproductive thinking. The client William engaged in ruminations about counterfactuals, i.e., how things could have been different, self-blame, and had intrusive images from the accident on the lake. All these things can in turn inhibit the possibility of PTG. So it is important to help the trauma survivor move into more productive, deliberate rumination, as we saw in the description of the PTG model in Chapter 1. This kind of rumination is generally focused on reconsidering core beliefs. Therefore it is important to look at how the shattering of the assumptive world can set the stage for this productive, deliberate rumination.

As we described in Chapter 1, the ways that traumatic events affect the assumptive world set in motion deliberate rumination in order to reconstruct a set of core beliefs that can account for the traumas of the past while being robust in the face of future traumas. In this way, the challenges to the assumptive world set the stage for PTG. The first part of the process is to examine the assumptive world that no longer appears to be useful given the traumatic events that have occurred. The beliefs related to the assumptive world have to do with identity, the future, and the kind of world this is or what to expect of the people in the world.

In the case of William, we see that his experience of Jeff's death challenged his sense of identity and future.

T: When we talked about how you felt about yourself for not being able to save Jeff, it seemed clear that you had never thought of yourself that way before.

C: Right, I had always thought I was capable, that I could handle things. I had confidence in myself. But, it wasn't just about not being able to save Jeff—I tipped the boat in the first place.

T: Yes, we talked about how that was the result of how you suddenly reacted to the emergency, and how Jeff was already hanging part way out as he was having the seizure.

C: It is still hard to feel good about myself in any way after this. I can't even look people in the eye any more. Like I said before, I don't even feel deserving of anything.

T: Of any good feeling toward you—from others or yourself.

Here the clinician keeps returning to empathic understanding in the midst of this evolving discussion of William's view of himself, and reviews again the issue of the circumstances of Jeff's death. The clinician makes an error in failing to make clear that the real issue is not only failing to save Jeff, but being involved in causing his death. This becomes part of the ensuing discussion.

C: Yeah. Even if I'm starting to think about it the way we said—that a lot of it was about the circumstances—I wonder what other people think. Maybe they blame me.

T: Is there any indication they do?

C: Actually I don't think so.

T: You told me about what Jeff's brother said to you.

C: Sometimes I wonder if he really meant it or was just saying the right thing.

T: The right thing?

C: Yeah, to make me feel better.

T: Maybe it's the right thing because it's true—you aren't to blame.

C: Yeah—I hope that's what he really thinks.

T: But is there any indication otherwise?

C: No, I guess not.

T: So Jeff's brother is OK with you. How much does his opinion matter to you?

C: A lot—he was his closest family.

T: OK. Is there anyone else who has given you a different opinion?

C: Just myself, I guess!

T: That's what it seems like. But you're a pretty tough prosecutor.

C: Yeah. That is sort of what I've been to myself. A prosecutor. Like I've charged myself...

T: Yes?

C: With... murder, I guess.

T: Hmm.

C: Maybe negligent homicide.

T: Do the facts support it?

Again, the therapist uses CBT methods to address William's view of himself as at least partly responsible for Jeff's death.

C: I guess not, as we talked about the circumstances.

T: But you are a pretty tough prosecutor.

C: Very. But I think I am starting to forgive myself for this.

T: I'm glad to hear it. How far along in that are you?

C: It really helped the way we went through the circumstances.

T: So, where does this leave you in terms of how you think of yourself? You said that you just don't see yourself in the same way before—so capable and being able to handle things.

The clinician takes the discussion away from the issue of negligent homicide to a broader consideration of the client's view of himself as capable. This gets into core beliefs that have been challenged. It would seem that viewing oneself as strong and capable is much superior to a view of oneself as unable to handle emergencies, panicking at the most crucial moments. In the case of William, the clinician has been working to change the view William has begun to adopt that he can no longer trust himself, that he panicked. But, given what happened on the lake, William can no longer see himself as capable in the way he did before. What is the possible advantage of a recognition that he is not immune to being taken by surprise and not having the best initial reaction to a situation? In this continuation of therapy with William, we see how this evolves.

C: You know, I don't know what of think of myself anymore. I'm not the guy I thought I was, but maybe not as bad as I was starting to think. But I don't know how to be around other people like this. Like I said, I have trouble looking people in the eye, and I don't think I deserve much.

T: Like you don't deserve some compassion?

C: No, I don't want to take that—it makes me feel worse. Why should I get that when Jeff's dead and his brother is suffering? I'd like to turn any of that compassion toward me to the people who really need it.

T: So you can handle this without that compassion, concern of other people for you.

C: Yeah, I think I can.

T: So, I start to think, "William says he doesn't need this concern from others, but he has come to talk with me."

C: OK, I see what you mean. I know this has messed me up, so you're a professional who can help me. I just don't need pity.

T: But we were talking about compassion and concern. Is that pity to you?

C: I guess not. You get me on these words, don't you?

T: I'm just trying to make sure I understand what you mean—I don't want to misunderstand.

C: Sometimes I have trouble understanding myself!

T: Part of explaining yourself to me means clarifying yourself to yourself. You have to put those thoughts into words. You know, William, going through this really makes you have to think about things you have not had to consider before. It is an uncomfortable process, but it could be useful for you.

The clinician takes the opportunity, given the statement the client makes about the difficulty understanding himself, to remark about the post trauma process the client is engaged in. There may be something useful in this. It may be premature for the clinician to make a remark about the possibility of PTG however, so this is left unsaid, only implied.

T: So anyway, accepting others' concern for you is not easy—or perhaps you don't see it as necessary—or perhaps you don't see yourself as deserving.

C: I guess all of those have some truth to them.

T: But this thing of having trouble looking people in the eye seems like a big deal to me. Like you have gone from feeling like you really don't need help, you can handle things, to you don't deserve, I don't know—concern? Respect?

C: Ooh. Respect is a big one with me. I want to be respected. But I feel humbled by this.

T: What is that like for someone like you?

C: It ain't easy.

T: Do you respect humility?

The clinician here puts the client in a bit of a bind, with the notion that respect, a "big one" for this client, can involve humility. This may allow the humility he is experiencing to be embraced. We may wonder what a more humble version of William might be like. Perhaps this could be an element of PTG.

C: Actually, yes, I do.

T: So you could respect humility in yourself.

C: I suppose so. But given the way I've gotten it, it's hard.

T: Maybe because the humility has been mixed in with self-blame. You know, that prosecutor is pretty tricky.

C: Yeah. If I could make sure those two are not mixed up I could live with myself. A more humble me. Might be OK. Might be a good thing.

T: Tell me what you're thinking about that.

C: Oh, I don't know. Maybe I've been a little cocky.

Here we see the seeds of PTG beginning to emerge into a changed perspective of himself. The clinician must be cautious to act as an expert companion in exploring these ideas. His job is to highlight them, help the trauma survivor embellish them and grow more familiar with them, and integrate them into a new sense of identity, the core beliefs he has about himself. The expert companion makes a bit of a judgment, about whether the beliefs that are emerging can better withstand future challenge. Core beliefs associated with PTG are those that lead to resilience. They allow the trauma survivor to navigate future events that are potentially traumatic with a sense of understanding and perspective, so there is not the necessity of reevaluating these core beliefs again. The question then becomes, what are core beliefs that are associated with resilience? We get a hint here as we follow the case of William. Consider the care the expert companion takes in exploring the nascent belief system that may be robust to future challenges, and the PTG process that has begun.

T: A little cocky? How so?

C: Maybe I thought I had it more together than I really have. No one has it all together. Well, I don't know maybe there is someone, but I guess I'm not him.

T: What would he look like?

C: I guess the things I used to think about myself. I can handle everything. I don't need help. Nothing can get to me too much. That sure isn't true—look at me here!

T: So, instead of that, what are you starting to think of yourself?

The way this question is asked is important. It highlights that there is a process going on, and it is just beginning. An alternative question might be "So, instead of that, who are you now?" But that doesn't allow for progression as much as the question asked here. PTG is a process that is likely just underway for William, and we don't want him to foreclose on it. Instead it is important for him to remain curious about himself.

C: Well, through all of this I am seeing that things can get to me. I don't like this word, but I guess it's true—it's like I'm more vulnerable. Vulnerable to life, I guess—to the things that can happen. Things can happen. Crazy things, at the drop of a hat. You never know what might happen, I guess. I guess I thought I had things under control, and I learned with Jeff that I didn't have them under control at all. Who knew Jeff would have a seizure? That's crazy. And right there, like you said, under some of the worst circumstances. I don't have it under control.

T: All these things about yourself, but also, more broadly, about how life, the circumstances of life, how that works—it looks different.

C: I mean, I suppose I knew I didn't really have control over things like another person's medical condition, or tornadoes, or something, but it is just different now. I know it in my gut. It is just more really true to me. It's hard to explain.

T: I think you are doing really well explaining it. Especially for something that we don't tend to talk about much.

C: Until something like this happens.

T: Right.

C: It forces your hand, now you have to think about it. At least I do. I guess I'm getting to be more a thinker. Maybe that's a change. I didn't really give much thought to stuff before. Just took things for granted in some way.

T: What did you take for granted?

C: Oh, I don't know. Pretty much everything. That everything is OK. Maybe I was an optimist, but I don't think so. I just didn't think I needed to worry, and life is going to work out. That whatever came along I could handle it. I guess I put a lot of faith in myself. I don't think that's a bad thing, and I still think I have faith in myself, but maybe not as much. I guess I'm rattled about that part.

T: Jeff's death has called it into question, at least, shaken up the system.

C: Yeah, that's a good way of putting it. You know, I have been thinking too that I've been selfish in all this. I've been thinking of myself, what's happening to me, and I need to think more about Jeff. I realized just the other day, that I am so concerned about myself, how bad I'm feeling, it's also like I forgot to really grieve for him. I think I have to be less focused on myself. I think that's something that needs changing.

T: You are taking a look at yourself very carefully as a result of all this.

C: I guess I never paid much attention to things like this before. Didn't have to, I suppose. It was going according to plan, pretty much.

T: Your life, you mean?

C: Yeah.

T: Of course, this was not part of the plan.

C: Hell, no.

T: It is not unusual for people to more deliberately think about what they believe about themselves and their lives as a result of things like this. In the long run it could help you.

C: It won't help Jeff, though.

T: It won't bring him back from the dead. So, now it's up to you, how you are going to live your life, given all that has happened.

C: I guess I have to decide a lot of things about that.

T: I think you are starting to do that.

Of course, by saying that Jeff's death has "shaken up the system," the clinician is clearly describing the idea of the shattered assumptive world, but in everyday, conversational language. We might also recognize that in addition to this "shaking" William is also having to consider what he believes about things much more deliberately than he has before. Perhaps this is what he means by "taking things for granted." Maybe what he took for granted was a belief system that had not been carefully considered. For many trauma survivors, the seismic event has led to deliberate consideration of core beliefs for the first time, rather than an undoing of a carefully constructed system based on a great deal of reflection. The deliberate rumination that is part of the PTG model described in Chapter 1 is what William in now engaged in. It is foreign territory to him, and an expert companion can play an important role in the exploration of this territory.

To this point, we have seen the importance to clients of understanding the ways that trauma responses can lead to PTG and resilience. These responses include the immediate reactions they had during the traumatic events, how they view these actions, and how they are coping in the aftermath of trauma. The role of the clinician is to use expert companionship to guide the trauma survivor into constructive views of him or herself based on this understanding of the normal responses people have to highly unusual and distressing events.

five
Emotion Regulation and Posttraumatic Growth

The model of growth that we described Chapter 1, includes an early aspect of the process of PTG that involves establishing an ability to regulate emotional reactions. This is important in the treatment of trauma symptoms generally and of PTSD in particular. However, we will not examine emotional regulation in the treatment of symptoms but we will consider the importance of this regulation capability in relation to PTG. There is overlap in the importance of therapy that focuses on emotional regulation in both standard trauma treatment and PTG facilitation, but we will focus on the latter.

The development of PTG requires the discussion of the traumatic stressor and its aftermath, incorporating elements of exposure treatment. In order to tolerate exposure to the story of the traumatic event and its effect on the survivor, clients will need to be able to regulate emotional reactions successfully, and to recognize that they have the tools necessary to approach discussion of the trauma, and to consider fully its implications. By achieving emotional regulation we are not encouraging avoiding emotionality, but approaching emotionality in a way that it is tolerable. PTG tends to be an experience that is creative, that is, the insights that we will later describe often occur in a way that is similar to the experience of creative ideas emerging into awareness—a bit surprising, and carrying emotional elements. We want clinicians to encourage survivors of traumatic events to retain the emotional aspects of the experience, not to sterilize it. The emotional power of trauma can be a catalyst for deep processing that can yield beneficial new perspectives. Earlier in the process, intrusive rumination tends to give way to a more deliberate, reflective rumination. At first the expert companion helps by introducing clients to ways to manage emotional distress, then helps show them ways to move from intrusive rumination to more deliberate rumination.

Evan was 17 when he died in a single car accident one mile from his home. His father had died of cancer when he was seven and his mother had not remarried. She was 49 and he was her only child.

He had obtained his restricted learner's permit when he was 16. She still did not allow him to carry anybody else in the car with him when he drove. She had drilled him repeatedly on the importance of driving carefully and defensively and, for his young age, Evan had been a good and wise driver.

He was not exceeding the 45 mile per hour speed limit when the car hit a puddle of water in the road. Police who investigated the accident suggested that the car may have hydroplaned, slid uncontrollably off the road and hit a tree. He was wearing a seat belt and the air bags deployed appropriately—but neither could save him. He died at the scene.

Four months after Evan's death his mother is struggling with many concerns, but is most uncomfortable with the highly emotional reactions she has several times a week.

C: I have these waves of grief that just crash over me unexpectedly. Sometimes they come because of something that is happening, but many times they come out of nowhere.
T: You didn't even realize you were that close to the ocean.
C: I know the ocean is always there, but sometimes it is high tide I guess.
T: Or maybe a hurricane.
C: A tsunami!

The clinician and the client work together here with a metaphor for her emotional experience of being out of control and overwhelmed.

T: So, sometimes it is really bad.
C: I am trying to get ready for work, and it just happens and I can't get myself together to be on time.
T: What exactly happens?
C: I just fall apart.
T: Meaning what?
C: I just feel these sobs coming up from down inside me, and I just burst into tears. And once it starts, well, sometimes it just keeps going. Sometimes I am late for work. Last week I got in the car and started driving anyway, and when I got to work, I was such a mess, I just turned around and went back home. Thank God they are pretty forgiving of me there.
T: Was there something that seemed to trigger this reaction, I mean specifically that day?

Although the clinician knows that these waves of grief can appear spontaneously, it is important to consider whether there are specific cues that are responsible for the reactions. In such a case, the client can be helped to develop new and more constructive responses to the cues.

C: It was one of those times it just comes out of the blue.

T: When you woke up, did you feel like you were going to cry?

C: Sometimes that happens—I wake up and it just hits me—Evan's dead! Like it is reality and not a dream. That happened that day—I guess it is just about every day.

T: So what did you do that morning?

C: I got up and started getting ready, the usual dragging myself into the day with my sadness. And that pit in my stomach.

T: That pit?

C: Like something bad is going to happen. I guess I always feel like something bad is going to happen now.

T: It already has.

C: The worst.

T: But let's get back to that day. What do you remember about getting ready?

C: Just the usual, getting a shower—sometimes I cry in there, but not that morning. Getting dressed and all. I get some juice and turn on the TV for the weather. Sometimes I do that and some story is on the news about a car accident and I just get upset and turn it off. But I don't think that happened that day. It's good when the weather comes on and I see it, and then I can turn it off before they start talking about all the bad stuff that has happened.

T: So, there was no trigger that day, anything specific you recall.

C: No, after that I just started to get ready to leave for work and I started feeling really bad.

T: The sadness?

C: Yes, just the thoughts of Evan.

T: What specifically did you start thinking?

C: He's dead and I'm going to work—what is the point to it? Maybe it's all pointless. I feel awful, why bother. What's next? What kind of horror is next in my life?

T: Part of you thinks life is going to be just pointless misery, and part expects even more horror.

Here it is clear that there is a cognitive aspect to the client's reactions. She starts to think that the life she is now living has no meaning without her son. This will need to be attended to therapeutically.

C: I guess so, but the worst has already happened like you say.

T: It seems that part of you that expects the bad is automatic.

C: It's just there.

T: Without even thinking, it just comes to you. All this stuff just comes to you automatically.

C: I'm controlled by my grief.

T: That's a good way of describing how it feels.

C: I'm just getting more of it every day. When will this stop? I hate living like this.

T: You hate living without Evan, and you hate having these feelings you are out of control of.

C: The whole thing is just pain, misery, anxiety, I just hate this. Sometimes I am not sure I want to go on like this. I need to know it will get better.

T: It will.

C: Really? When?

T: The when is hard to say, but it will be gradual, so you may hardly notice it for a while. If you look back to how you were and consider how you are now, you may notice some changes.

C: I think I'm getting worse. I was calmer before.

T: Grief often works this way. An initial period of shock and numbness gives way to more recognition of the reality of this, the permanence of it.

The clinician chooses here to address the sense the client has that she is getting worse. This will not be a useful thought if a goal is for her to gain confidence in her ability to manage her emotions. So, a bit of psychoeducation about grief is in order. This demonstrates how flexibility is needed by clinicians. Instead of proceeding with the emotional reactions, the clinician chooses to address this mother's view that the apparently meaningless life she is living will only get worse. Grief typically abates over time, so the clinician has an empirical basis for his prediction (Alam, Barrera, D'Agostino, Nicholas, & Schneiderman, 2012; Feigelman, Jordan, & Gorman, 2009).

C: Yeah, I was just a zombie at the funeral. I had all that Xanax.

T: You do need a way to try to regulate all this emotion that comes over you so you don't just feel like you are a victim of it. We need to develop a strategy for making this grief response less automatic.

C: That would be good. I mean, I know I have to grieve, I *want* to grieve for Evan. He deserves that. I would feel bad not grieving.

T: That's why you stopped taking the Xanax.

C: I was too numb.

This acknowledgement of the importance of the grief itself is supported by the clinician, but the next statement tends to negate it, so the client wonders about the use of the medication.

T: Now you feel too upset sometimes.

C: Do you think I should take the Xanax again?

T: Not necessarily. We have other things we can do.

The clinician does not want to encourage use of this particular medication, but this does not mean that medications are to be totally avoided. Sometimes medications can help clients to feel less controlled and overwhelmed by their emotions (Hensley, 2006; Shear & Mulhare, 2008). But it is best for clients to attribute at least part of their success to their own efforts (Wachtel, 2011).

C: Like what?

T: OK, first I want to explain something about this grief process. It is messy and doesn't follow neat stages like some people have said.

C: Yeah, the stages of grief—I read about that online—shock, and anger, depression, or is it bargaining next?

T: Well, my point is that it doesn't usually break down into these clear stages. But initially there can be some kind of self-protective numbness and the recognition of the reality of it, and a deeper sense of being wounded can follow. That's why you can feel like it is getting worse as you grieve.

The therapist returns to the issue of why the client may be feeling worse because of the increasing intensity of her emotional response. But it is important to not allow the client to see this as regression. Also, there is a reference to stages of grief, and the clinician uses his expertise about the research literature to let this mother know that she does not need to concern herself with a rigid version of this concept and worry about the degree to which she is meeting expectations of following a series of stages in her grieving (Bonanno, 2009; Doka, 1995; Konigsberg, 2011).

C: So that is normal? I guess that's a stupid way to put it—none of this is normal, but you know what I mean?

T: Yes, that's how it often goes. You are moving through this, and nothing you have told me seems out of the ordinary given the terrible circumstances.

C: I'm still basically OK.

T: Although you feel broken, you are OK. You are a grieving mother, and this is what grieving mothers go through.

C: It's hell.

T: Yes.

C: So, I just have to go through it.

T: Yes you do, but there are some things that can help you. So, let's get to that.

At this point, these simple statements reflect the fundamental truth of dealing with trauma. The trauma survivor has to go through it but there are things that can help.

C: Good.

T: Remember how we talked last time about the trauma response that is part of your grief?

C: The fight or flight? Yes.

T: It's another self-protective thing like the numbness was. We are built to try to protect ourselves physically and psychologically. So you have been reliving every day the fact of Evan's death and the memories of it.

C: Oh yes—I just find myself hearing the doorbell ring—when the cops showed up and told me. Sometimes I think I am actually hearing it when I am home. A couple of times I have gone to the door. Sometimes I don't go to the door, I am afraid it's happening again. This time my husband or something.

T: These are ways your mind is attempting to come to terms with all this, trying to master the situation by going through it over and over.

C: It's like my mind can't get it.

T: It's too much.

C: So my mind is working on it.

T: Right. But we want to help you get your mind off automatic pilot and to be more under your direction. So, one thing we need to do is to give you a way to soothe your automatic response of anxiety and a sense that something terrible will happen again, and that you had better be ready for it. We need to help you calm down from all that.

The clinician introduces the concept that managing the anxiety is a basic task and that there are simple tools for accomplishing it. This appears to be turning from the expert companionship model of trauma intervention we have been describing, to a model that puts the clinician in a position of leadership. The form of expertise that emerges in this session involves more psychoeducation and skills training in regulation of emotions and thinking. This leadership must be done in a fashion that accommodates the survivors' specific experiences and tracks carefully their willingness and ability to use these tools. There is still companionship in this approach.

C: That would be great.

T: Fortunately, there is something simple we can start with—breathing.

C: Well—I know how to do that!

T: Yes, but we are going to practice breathing in a way that helps you so you don't escalate into these feelings of being overwhelmed. Here is what I want you to do. I will show you. Just get comfortable in your chair, with your arms at your sides, not crossed over your chest, have your feet on the floor, and breathe in a nice, full, deep breath through your nose like this (talking while demonstrating), hold it for just a count of one, and then let it go through your mouth. I am not pushing it, just letting it go. Then I am going to wait. I am waiting to see when I need another breath. I won't take any little breaths, just these deep ones. I am still waiting—I can wait a long time because of this deep breath. OK, now I am ready to breathe again, and I am going to repeat this (going through another sequence). OK?

C: OK, let me try it.

T: OK, remember to take that deep breath through your nose, filling your lungs with air, hold it, now let go naturally, without pushing. Now wait. See when your body tells you it is time to breathe. No little breaths.

C: I'm waiting.

T: Good.

C: OK, time to breathe again. (She goes through the sequence.)

T: Looking good. Keep going. (The client continues through a couple more sequences).

C: Yeah, that's OK. That's going to help?

T: What does it feel like?

C: I definitely feel more relaxed.

T: That's what we want.

C: Yes.

The problem with this breathing exercise is that it may seem too simple to be an effective tool for dealing with something that seems so powerful to the client. A more "high tech" explanation may be in order so the client will be convinced, even though her own experience indicated that the method was helping.

T: See, that fight or flight response we talked about—the ways your body is responding to get ready for action? You can't change it through an act of will for the most part. You can't direct your heart rate to slow, blood pressure to drop and so forth. But you can directly control your breathing. You are slowing your breathing by breathing deeply, and that will affect these other systems. This breaks down this sympathetic nervous system response. When you start to remember Evan's death, this gets activated, so we need for you to have a way to counteract it. Like when I just said "Evan's death," what did you feel?

C: That pit in my stomach just kind of jumped up.

T: Right—that's the beginning of this response. But when that kind of thing happens, you can breathe.

C: OK—anytime that happens.

This simple exercise accomplished a few things. It does produce relaxation, as described to the client. It is also gives the client something to do when her anxiety increases rather than being a passive victim of it. It also interrupts the pattern the client lives that produces the escalating anxiety.

T: Actually, I'd like you to practice this breathing twice a day for about five minutes each time. Once in the morning perhaps before work, and once later on, maybe when you get home. I just want you to get really familiar with it, and also to kind of set yourself to this calmer state a couple times a day. You can also use it whenever you want. It's cheap, portable, no side effects. OK?

C: I'll try.

T: OK, we will review it next time to see how you are doing. This is going to help you get off automatic pilot with the trauma and grief—now you have a tool to use.

C: I sure want to feel better, not all better, of course.

T: Of course. This doesn't make things all better. Nothing can. But you can start to feel less victimized by it when you have a way to start to manage it.

C: Like when I start talking about it here and start to cry and just get all messed up.

T: And then it's hard to think…

C: I can't think straight anymore, I'm just in that world of "Evan's dead."

T: Yeah, it will be good to be able to think and talk and be able to deal with everything this has brought into your life. All the things that have changed.

This talk about thinking straight about her loss and its aftermath is setting the stage for the cognitive work to follow and the focus on PTG that can come with it.

C: Yeah, I need a way to keep calm so I can talk about it, think straight about it. And get to work, too.

T: That's right, your life has changed and we need to take a look at what it's going to be.

Again, this is a suggestion that the clinician and trauma survivor will be reviewing what has happened, but also what can happen in the future—what life can be. In that, there is possibility for PTG. These are suggestions that may go almost unnoticed but are important to say in order to orient the client to the next phases of the therapy and the possibilities for PTG.

C: I just feel like a mess at this point.

T: I think having a method to deal with some of this anxiety and pain, to soothe yourself a bit might allow you to see that you are not just a mess. There are other things we can do to help you through this as well, but this breathing exercise alone can be surprisingly helpful.

The clinician encourages the use of the slow breathing exercise based on indications that it can help with anxiety (McCaul, Solomon, & Holmes, 1979; Sakakibara & Hayano, 1996; Yuen & Sander, 2010). The clinician gives the message that the client is not just a "mess" despite the feelings of the moment. These are consistent messages about possibility and success at managing the traumatic aftermath. At the same time the clinician, as an expert companion, is helping the client with tools to manage better; there is an emphasis on understanding that this is difficult and the trauma survivor is showing courage and having success. In the next session, the client reports the following.

C: I have been doing the breathing almost every day, and I really like it. It helps.

T: Good!

C: I can feel I am a little more calm.

T: You have been practicing twice a day?

C: Most days.

T: And using it at other times?

C: Yes, I had a couple of those times I was trying to get to work and I was really upset. I did the breathing in my car in the parking lot one day before work, and I was able to get calm and go in. I think it might have been a day I turned around and went back home otherwise. So, I like it.

T: I am glad you are practicing it. That's what it takes.

This idea that practice produces useful change somehow gets lost on many clients. It is important to encourage clients to try out new methods in their time outside of therapy in order to maximize the benefits of the therapy sessions.

C: What about those other things you said I could do, what are those?

T: Well, one is a visualization exercise I can guide you through that many people also find helpful in being able to soothe themselves. We can practice that.

C: OK.

T: All right, I will just ask you to close your eyes for this one, and we will start with your breathing exercise and then you just need to listen to my instructions.

The instructions for this exercise involve a lot of passive and permissive wording so the client never gets the sense of doing anything wrong in the exercise. It is not like much of what is done in "guided imagery" where the clinician chooses the images. These images suggested in guided imagery can also have a strong cultural bias, as indicated in a review of guided imagery scripts found in the literature by La Roche, Batista and D'Angelo (2011). These authors obtained 393 scripts, which demonstrates a range of possibilities that clinicians have suggested might be useful with clients. With trauma survivors in particular, clinicians do not know which images may be comforting and which may be relaxing, so it is better to let the client choose the image. The word "relax" is not used so that the client does not feel that anything is being demanded, and if they are having difficulty relaxing it is a mistake. After a few moments of the breathing exercise with which the client has already had success, the clinician continues with these imagery instructions.

T: Now I want you to let come to mind a place that is very comfortable and peaceful to you. It could be a place you have been to, a place you would like to go, or a place that is purely of your imagination. When a place like this begins to come to mind, I want you to raise one hand to let me know.

Notice that in these instructions the wording is passive—let come to mind and permissive—any place the client wants. To let clients experience success even when they may have some trouble with the image, the wording is "when a place *like this begins* to come to mind." Finally, to allow the client to stay connected with the experience, the clinician asks for a response non-verbally. Giving much of this exercise over to the trauma survivor is another act of companionship. The clinician trusts the client to be able to manage this new way of emotional regulation. The expert companion does not even ask about the client's "place" they have chosen. Whatever it is, it is a choice that the client can be trusted with, and not asking about it can make it private and special, and perhaps then, having more power.

On very rare occasions, clients may be made acutely anxious by the use of such an exercise. Some may cry. Giving up control and freely allowing themselves to surrender to the clinician's instructions, or beginning to visualize something can bring them face-to-face with memories or emotions that they have been suppressing. The clinician should then stop the exercise and explore the survivor's experience. For these clients, the breathing exercise alone is more appropriate.

> T: Good. Now I would like you to notice the colors of things. You may notice anything you would like, but let colors begin to come to your mind.

After a pause for about 30 seconds, the clinician offers another prompt that focuses the client on another sensory aspect of her experience with this place in order to make it more vivid. Intervals of about 30 seconds or so are used between all prompts to allow the client to use them with the image they are working with.

> T: Notice the shapes of things in this place. Allow yourself to trace the outlines of whatever you may wish to notice.

Again, the instructions are passive, using the word "notice" rather than "look" in order to keep the experience as non-demanding as possible, and therefore to minimize any sense of failure or anxiety. Another instruction that is meant to do this is repeated two of three times during the exercise.

> T: If at any point you find yourself distracted, by a noise, a thought, or a sensation, that's OK. Just let yourself go back to this peaceful, comfortable place.

These experiences of distraction are virtually certain to happen. The experience of being able to toggle back and forth between distracting or disturbing thoughts and something more comforting is an important skill that we want the trauma survivor to develop. A similar kind of ability to manage rumination or distraction may be developed in mindfulness training (Jain, et al., 2007; Semple, 2010) and meditation practices (Hasenkamp, Wilson-Mendenhall, Duncan, & Barsalou, 2012).

T: Notice the texture of things. What would it feel like to run your fingertips over the surface of something in this place that you would like to touch.

Another 30 seconds is allowed to pass in order for the client to work with this part of the experience.

T: Notice the temperature in this place. It may be pleasantly warm or cool, but notice the feel of the air on your skin.

In order to allow for different possibilities, the instruction allows for "warm or cool" which are words that can each connote something "pleasant."

T: Notice any sounds in this place. There may be certain pleasant sounds, or it may be very quiet.

Again, this wording allows for the various possibilities since we know nothing of the place the client has conjured up.

T: Notice any pleasant fragrances in this place.

The word "fragrances" is used rather than "smells" since fragrance has a more positive connotation. By the time all these sensory prompts are used with gaps of about 30 seconds or so, and the visualization has followed the breathing exercise, about 10 minutes has passed. To end this exercise, the client is given a gradual return from the pleasant place. She is given an initial description and then the process begins.

T: In a moment I am going to ask you to begin to open your eyes. I will count from three to one, and each time your eyes will open a little more. We will start with three, and I would like you let your eyes open the slightest little bit, just allowing a little light in the bottom of your eyes, and your eyelids are just hanging there, feeling heavy, and then you may allow your eyes to close once more.

The passive wording continues with words such as "let" and "allow." The mention of the heavy eyelids confirms what the client will be experiencing as they are opening their eyes in this fashion.

T: Now, with number two, I would like you to let your eyes open a little bit more, letting in a little more light, so that you may see things but they are blurry and out of focus. Now you may let your eyes close once more.

Between each number, the instructions are delayed about five or ten seconds, to allow the sense of comfort to be re-established.

T: Now with number three, I would like you to let your eyes to gradually begin to open, and as they do so, you will let in a little more light at a time, and things will begin to come into focus, until you are back here in this room with me.

After giving clients an opportunity to get re-oriented, the clinician can ask if the client was comfortable with such exercises or if they had any aspects of it that were more difficult. It is not necessary for clients to have success with every sensory prompt. These are simply ways to help clients to fully engage in the experience of being comfortable in an atmosphere of their choosing and construction. Clients may sometimes say that they experienced more than one "place" and had trouble staying with one. In responding to this and other difficulties, the clinician continues the approach used throughout the exercise, i.e., it is OK for clients to do whatever they prefer, though they may find that a particular place is preferred on a particular occasion. The important message for clients who are having trouble managing emotional reactions is that they are doing well with the exercise, and that the difficulties they may encounter are common and constitute an opportunity to learn methods to become more proficient at moving from tension to calmness.

There are a number of methods that can be used to help clients to reduce anxiety and ruminative processes associated with traumatic events, including various relaxation, meditative and hypnotic procedures (Bormann, Thorp, Wetherell, Golshan, & Lang, 2012; Descilo, 2010; Spiegel, 2010). It is useful for clinicians to be competent in different procedures so that clients who do not do well with one type of procedure can be helped with another.

Although the emotional regulation introduced here is meant to be a practical method for this grieving mother to manage anxiety, other clients may be particularly good students of such methods and they may get more than enhanced emotional regulation alone. Some clients have said that learning such techniques changed their lives. They practiced these techniques consistently, and found that they were therefore able to manage any situation. They gained enormous confidence and peace of mind, knowing that no matter what happened they would be able to use their breathing tool to good effect. One active duty soldier reported that he used this in the middle of a firefight when he was beginning to panic, and he concluded that if it could be effective then, that it was completely reliable. Knowing that you have the strength to handle any difficulty is one of the domains of PTG that can be affected by learning this emotion management tool. It appears that we are just beginning to learn about the pervasive influences the use of these types of interventions may have on our clients' lives (Kemeny, et al., 2012).

Another aspect of this client's difficulties is the thought that her son is dead—"Evan's dead." The clinician noted that she might have had a reaction to his mentioning this, and indeed she said that the pit in her stomach "jumped up." Let us turn to the cognitive regulation that can be a useful focus along with the regulation of the survivor's emotions. In the process, it will become more apparent how PTG facilitation is involved.

T: The thought "Evan's dead" seems to be something that almost always unnerves you.

C: Always.

T: What happens to you when you think that?

C: I get the pit in my stomach.

T: Is there anything else you think then?

C: Oh yeah—it starts a bunch of things.

T: Like what?

C: I start thinking of what I could have done to prevent it, or how it might not have happened.

This is the counterfactual thinking common to many survivors of traumatic stressors (Gilbar, Plivazky, & Gil, 2010). Trauma survivors attempt to counter the factual reality of what has happened by imaging another narrative where something prevents it. This kind of thinking may sometimes give brief satisfaction, but then reality becomes apparent again and a cascade of unpleasant feelings and ruminative thoughts may follow. This intrusive rumination—automatic and unpleasant—must eventually give way to a more deliberate, reflective form of thinking. The clinician tries to aid in this process.

T: What do you find yourself thinking?

C: I wish I hadn't let him go out that day. I knew it was raining and maybe he shouldn't drive because it was slippery. I wish I had listened to my intuition or whatever.

T: Whatever?

C: I don't know what it was, but I had a bad feeling and I overrode it. I told myself I was being silly. Overprotective.

T: And you think, if only you had paid attention to the bad feeling.

C: You know what I wonder?

T: What?

C: That feeling was so strong. I wonder if it was a message from God.

T: A warning from God.

C: Sounds crazy to you, I bet.

T: No, it doesn't.

Working with clients who have faced traumatic events introduces clinicians to all sorts of powerful experiences that are reported by clients. We think that expert companions become open to the possibilities of these experiences. They are quite real to our clients. A good example can be found in a book by novelist and playwright Reynolds Price, who describes a mystical experience while being treated for spinal cancer (Price, 1994).

C: Well, I am a strong believer, and I think it might have been a message.

T: It may have been. But you didn't heed it.

This may seem harsh, but the clinician is in close contact with the flow of this conversation, anticipating that this is exactly the mother's point. Her response validates this.

C: To my everlasting regret.
T: You imagine then, if you had heeded this, none of this would have happened and Evan would have been alive.
C: That little decision changed everything. I am so angry with myself. Why didn't I just stop him?
T: You try to answer that question?
C: It just seemed like not that big a deal, realistically, even though I had that feeling.
T: So you were being realistic.
C: I thought so at the time.
T: I'll bet there are many situations where you might have had a feeling you overrode and nothing bad happened.
C: It's hard to remember.
T: Because nothing bad happened. It wasn't memorable.
C: Probably so. I wonder if I ignored other messages from God. I don't know, maybe this one was special.

Here the client is musing about what might have happened. The expert companion allows for the client's interpretation, that she may have received a message from God, but also loosens up her thinking to consider that she might have ignored other "feelings" or "messages" in the past. This looseness can allow clients to work together on getting past the counterfactuals, regrets, and self-blame, that all can contribute to trauma survivors having difficulty with forgiving themselves, and ultimately finding elements of PTG in the experience.

T: I wonder if we will be able to figure this out.
C: I am not sure how to do that.
T: I am not sure either.
C: I have been thinking about it a lot.
T: Getting anywhere with it?
C: Not much.
T: You know, I think at some point you will have to decide what to believe. You will need to choose the thing that right now makes most sense to you, or what you prefer to believe about it. Who is to say what is right or wrong in this.
C: I guess there is no way to prove what that was all about.
T: Not that I can figure.
C: So I can think whatever I want about it.
T: Yes, but it might be useful to consider the implications. So, if you choose to believe that God tried to give you a message that you shouldn't let Evan drive, and you disregarded it, then what do you think next?

C: God might be angry with me?

T: That's what you think?

C: I'm not sure. Well, I think if God knew this was about to happen, then why didn't He stop it?

T: He was counting on you to stop it, so He could have stopped it instead?

C: I think so.

T: Not sure?

C: I am not sure how these things work—does God control everything? Sometimes we pray and things don't go our way. Or here, God warned me but let this tragedy happen. It's not clear to me how this works.

T: It's not clear what kind of God you believe in.

C: I guess I never had to think so seriously about it before.

Together with this bereaved mother, the expert companion is wandering through a maze of questions about God, the degree to which God is omnipotent, and responsibility for the son's death. The therapist does not have answers, but instead encourages a process of rumination that they can do together. This is like a guided rumination, a more constructive way to think other than the intrusive rumination that the mother engaged in before.

The mother remarks that she has never had to think about these things before. Trauma often sets off this reflection on the assumptive world. These core beliefs may be a poorly articulated set of beliefs, or a well-articulated set of beliefs that no longer stand up to the scrutiny that traumatic circumstance has forced. The clinician must be patient in the consideration of these beliefs, while guiding the trauma survivor through a more constructive and deliberate process of rumination. The expert companion also works within the client's framework, understanding the client's general worldview and belief system. In this case, religious beliefs appear to be important, and these will be discussed in more detail in Chapter 8.

As we mentioned in Chapter 2, it appears to be commonplace for people to operate with belief systems that include certain benign illusions (Taylor, 1989). In this case the client maintained the illusion that her son was not in danger, and now it seems this was not such a benign perspective. But, if she had had a constant concern about his safety, she would be anxious and suspicious—not a comfortable situation for her or her son. Now, after his death, she needs to reconsider the belief system that supported this view. In doing so, she may begin to develop other beliefs that some might think are illusory. We recommend that expert companions should be accepting of these beliefs as long as they are self-protective and are not indicative of an inability to accept reality, i.e., denial. Even then, the clinician should tread lightly and recognize that self-protection is especially important for trauma survivors whose core beliefs have been challenged unlike ever before. Clinicians need to use their judgment to determine when to challenge and when to support emerging beliefs. Let us consider again how this is done with Evan's mother.

T: This has forced you to think about it—to think about God and how he operates in this world.

C: Yes, so I am thinking that if God was giving me a message, why didn't He go ahead and save Evan?

T: And you are searching for an answer. Or you may decide to see the situation differently.

C: Like maybe God wasn't giving me a message. But still, where was He when Evan had his wreck? Why didn't He save him?

T: Does God save people in these situations?

C: Right—another question I don't know the answer to. He seems to save some and not others.

T: What do you choose to believe about that?

C: You know, right now I am driving myself nuts with all of this.

T: What are you going to do? You know, it may not be necessary to figure all this out right now. There are no proofs to these things, and you have choice about what to believe, or not. And you may change these ideas.

C: It's all right to just live with it? To not know, really?

T: It might be better right now than trying to force the issue, when you may not be ready. Sometimes it is good to lay back and let a problem just be, for a while, instead of pounding away at it. You ever had the experience of trying to remember something and couldn't, then later on it came to you out of the blue?

C: Yes, maybe this could be like that. But this seems more complicated.

T: Seems to be. But it could work in a similar way. We just know that you haven't been able to sort it out to this point.

C: I think I'm going to just live with not understanding it. At least for now. For now I don't know what to choose, as you say. So, I think I'll choose to say I don't know, but that what will it change? Nothing about Evan. What I really want to believe is that God is taking care of him. In heaven He can take care of him just fine. He's running the show up there. On earth, us poor mortals are screwing things up, not knowing what to believe or what to do, how to interpret His messages, and so on. So, what if I just believe that Evan is in God's hands, and I will never know what that feeling was about that day. Just something that might have been an intuition, or a message, I don't know. But it was not convincing enough to tell him, "you're not going out."

T: Sounds like that might be a way to look at this that allows you to feel a little more comfortable and not continue to distress yourself with unanswerable questions. Maybe some time in the future you may be able to return to these questions when they don't stir up so much hurt and pain. Or maybe this resolution will work fine for you throughout your life. What we do know is that you have now come into contact with some big questions about living life in a world where we wonder about the presence of God. You will probably take these questions seriously, whether or not you discern some answers. This is what has happened because of having to deal with Evan's death.

The expert companion is careful not to say something potentially offensive such as "Evan's death has given you a chance to consider these questions." Instead, the statement becomes "This is what has happened because of having to deal with Evan's death." Being very careful with words can be especially important in working with trauma survivors, although this is certainly true of all clinical work (Wachtel, 2011). It is important in circumstances such as the death of a child to make a distinction between the event itself, and needing to cope with it. We are focused here on the aftermath of traumatic events and what can be done to manage the aftermath. In this managing, PTG can evolve.

Note that the clinician implies change here, and that the change might be in the direction of PTG. This is the subtle message of change at this point, a labeling of the process that is underway, even if we cannot say where it will take this client. The clinician sees in the client certain possibilities she may not see in herself. She may only see that she is trying to find a way to survive her pain. The expert companion looks down the road and points out there may be relief ahead, but even more than that.

six
Constructive Self-disclosure and Redevelopment of Relationships

We continue to use the PTG model described in Chapter 1 as a guide for our clinical work, turning now to self-disclosure. Traumatic events often present survivors with a dilemma. The experience of the events warrants telling someone else about them yet, in the telling, the survivor may fear that others will betray confidences, fail to empathize, or be critical. Self-disclosure becomes difficult, and may be avoided. Yet, this disclosure may be crucial to the trauma survivors' ability to understand their own experiences, as they try to articulate these experiences in a way that allows them to obtain support and understanding from others.

The study of self-disclosure in psychology was pioneered by Sidney Jourard (Jourard & Lasakow, 1958), and his seminal work produced a large literature that has clarified some of the circumstances under which self-disclosure is likely to happen and its effects on the person doing the disclosing and receiving the disclosures. In recent years, the literature has focused on the disclosure of distressing emotional information, either verbally (Kahn & Hessling, 2001; Kahn, Hucke, Bradley, Glinski, & Malak, 2012), or through writing (Pennebaker, 1997). Generally, it appears that self-disclosure of emotional and personal information is related to being psychologically and physically healthy. Persons with metacognitive ease or fluency are more likely to disclose distressing information (Alter & Oppenheimer, 2009). A meta-analysis of 146 experimental written disclosure studies indicated that these disclosures are useful for promoting psychological and physical health and that this effect may result from exposure processes, more than from cognitive processing (Frattaroli, 2006).

Self-disclosure is the basic building block of psychotherapy. Without self-disclosure therapy is impossible. It might also be said that without self-disclosure interpersonal relationships are stunted, unsatisfying, and perhaps ultimately impossible to sustain. The emotional heightening caused by trauma makes disclosures more necessary and perhaps more likely, and posttraumatic distress can drive people to seek out others to whom to disclose. When informal sources are not available, paid listeners, i.e., psychotherapists are sought.

In many trauma-focused therapies, self-disclosure is a primary element. Exposure therapies often require detailed accounts of trauma experiences as part of the exposure, and cognitive processing therapies require such disclosures in order to thoroughly comprehend what actually occurred and to correct misconceptions about the traumatic experiences (Resick, & Shnicke, 1993). These disclosures may be difficult for both the trauma survivor to recount and for a clinician to hear.

However, the expert companion needs to listen to heart-wrenching stories without flinching, and at the same time exhibit empathy for the survivor. With empathy the expert companion asks questions and makes comments that encourage the client to tell the details of the story, and perhaps to include elements of the story that would otherwise be forgotten or be assumed to be too disturbing for a listener. The expert companion must also remember to be sensitive to the choices the trauma survivor must make in telling personal stories, and not be demanding of more disclosure than is useful. It is not necessary for every detail to be shared and for every distressing element to be disclosed. Some things may be better left unsaid, but it requires an astute, empathetic listener to determine this. The clinician's focus should include the traumatic event itself, but also the aftermath and how the client is managing this part of the story. So the expert companion encourages discussion of the whole story, as will be discussed in more detail in Chapter 7.

With an enhanced ability to self-disclose, trauma survivors are in a position to rework their way of relating to other people. Openness with other people is not only about disclosing facts and events, but about an ability to feel more emotionally open and less concerned with the judgment of others about them. This may not come immediately and will need the support and reassurance from an expert companion to achieve. But comfort with oneself and one's trauma history is liberating and produces confidence and greater empathy.

Consider how this evolves in the case of a survivor of rape. Julie is a 30-year-old single woman who was raped while on a date with a man she had known for about a month. He was part of a social group she was involved with and her decision to report this rape to the police caused great turmoil in her social network. The following discussion occurred during the fourth session of therapy. At this point she had described the rape itself and how she had decided to report it even though she knew some people would be upset with her for doing so.

C: This is getting to be a real mess with everyone having their opinion about it. You know, I have gone from not wanting anyone to know and thinking I would just keep it a secret, to it being, like, a major topic of conversation for everyone.

T: More than you bargained for?

C: The whole thing is more than I bargained for. Going out with Craig sure was, that creep. And now I have to deal with all this.

T: All the talk.

C: It's all over Facebook, and everyone thinks they know what really happened when they weren't there. A lot of people think Craig's a great guy and he couldn't have done it, and they are calling me all kinds of names. You know, I thought it would be a lot of guys who might do this, but it's girls, too. People I thought were my friends, who really know me. It's so depressing, and kind of... well, all kinds of things.

T: Like?

C: Embarrassing of course, and it makes me really mad what people say, and kind of scary.

T: Scary, like...

C: I don't know what I'll get when I see people. I've been avoiding going places. And Craig's out there on bail and acting like it's all just ridiculous.

T: You've shown a lot of courage through this.

C: Sometimes I don't feel very courageous.

T: That's the fear in you.

C: Yeah, this whole thing is crazy, scary. I can't believe it's me.

T: But here you are, and you decided to fight.

C: I did, and sometimes I wonder.

T: Whether it's worth it.

C: Yeah.

At this point, we can see what has happened in Julie's life because of her decision to disclose the rape. Her relationships have been in turmoil and she has wondered whether she made the right choice in reporting the rape to police. The expert companion simply encourages her to tell this part of the story, and now has a choice. The focus could be on her fear and doubt, or if the clinician wishes to be a growth oriented expert companion, the other side of the equation can be highlighted.

T: You say "sometimes."

C: What?

This deliberately ambiguous statement on the part of clinician is meant to attract the client's attention, so that the message about personal strength in this circumstance is clearly heard.

T: You say "sometimes" rather than all the time. Sometimes you wonder, and sometimes you don't feel very courageous. So I guess sometimes you are also quite sure of yourself?

C: Well, I don't really think I did the wrong thing. You know we talked about it pretty thoroughly didn't we?

T: I think we did.

C: And I really don't think I could do differently.

T: Imagine going out and seeing Craig around, knowing what he did to you.

C: That I couldn't handle. That would be awful. But he's kind of doing that now, acting like he's innocent and I'm some sort of—I don't know what. Why would I falsely accuse him of this? I don't know how anyone could figure that—it just doesn't make sense. Would I want to cause myself all this trouble?

T: Right, if people gave it some thought…

C: They would see it!

T: I guess some people thought they really knew Craig, and can't reconcile this with the Craig they thought they knew.

C: You know, I just thought something I hadn't thought before when you said that. I was just the same. I mean, I thought I knew Craig, too. I thought he was safe. I'd never go out with a potential rapist. So I guess in some strange way I see where they are coming from.

The conversation has veered a bit from the strength Julie is showing by reporting this rape and cooperating with the police investigation. But this insight is useful and potentially important in Julie's understanding of what is happening in her relationships, so the expert companion has the flexibility to follow.

T: Remember, you figured that some people wouldn't believe you.

C: Especially with a date rape and all, and the circumstances.

T: So, maybe some of this isn't so surprising?

C: I guess not, but it's just worse than I really thought, you know? I just didn't think about how bad it was going to be.

T: But you still think the alternative, keeping quiet, would have been even more difficult to tolerate.

C: Right. That son of a bitch, why did he have to do this? Why did he put me in this mess?

T: That's the point—he didn't have to do this. But he chose to.

C: He should at least of thought what a mess he'd cause himself.

T: I guess he didn't figure on your strength. That you'd stand up to him.

C: I couldn't fight him off, but I'm still fighting anyway. Rough sex, bullshit. Telling people I liked rough sex. Unbelievable how he's trying to save his own skin. First he rapes me, then…

T: He's still doing it.

C: Exactly!

T: Your indignation helps sometimes, doesn't it.

C: That's right. I am NOT going to back down on this. I can tell people the truth. They're just going to have to deal with it. Craig and everybody else. It's the truth. Deal with it!

T: Do you see yourself differently now that you are going through all this?

C: What do you mean?

Again, the expert companion has stayed close to the client's experience, and has helped her to label and articulate it. It appears that the statement that the rapist is "still doing it," by trying to portray her as a liar who simply wanted rough sex, allows her to disclose more of her indignation, and this in turn reassures her of her strength and the correctness of her decision. Now some PTG can be highlighted.

> T: Well, what words would you have used to describe yourself before this, and what ones now?
> C: I guess before I would have said I was nice, and kind, and a little shy, and fun-loving.
> T: Have you felt that way lately?
> C: Wow, no, not at all.
> T: So, what do you see in yourself now?
> C: Determined, really determined. And pretty tough, yeah, tough, I guess.
> T: I thought you said you were scared?
> C: Sometimes, remember?
> T: On yeah, right, only sometimes.
> C: The rest of the time I'm being pretty tough. I never really thought of myself that way before. Determined, maybe. I could see myself as determined. But tough, I don't know.
> T: It looks like dealing with people about this has helped your toughness come out.

In this segment, the clinician has Julie look at personal characteristics she may not have noticed in herself before, or personal characteristics she has developed. It is likely that some nascent characteristics have developed due to the demands of the situations she has confronted. The last thing she said about determination being a part of her before the rape, but maybe not toughness, prompts the clinician to come back with a wording about toughness that attributes some nascent toughness to her. This is more complimentary of her, that it is part of her, but only needed to "come out" under these extraordinary circumstances.

> C: Maybe so. I'm tougher than I thought.
> T: It's taken that to stand up for yourself and say exactly what really happened.
> C: It was when I decided to do it, it was, like, I called the police, and the words wouldn't come out at first. I had to really force myself.
> T: And of course you had to answer a lot of questions.
> C: How weird and embarrassing.
> T: But you did it.
> C: Yes, I did.
> T: For many rape survivors, telling the story is as traumatizing as the rape itself.
> C: That's right. And this just keeps going on.
> T: But you don't just keep talking about it. You have to choose…

C: Yeah, I choose who to talk to about it now. Really carefully. But I can say it when I need to. When I came in here and you asked me what had happened, I had told the police and my sister, but nobody else the whole thing. And I was thinking, what do I want to say about this? I didn't really want to say all the details.

T: You had just come in, just met me. So, I wouldn't expect you to tell about everything, necessarily.

C: Yeah, and when I said I was raped, you said I could say whatever I wanted about it. So I was choosing, and thinking I'll just tell enough to give you the overview, as it were. I wasn't even sure I could talk to a man about it, but I trusted what my sister said. And she was right, you're OK.

T: I'm glad she was right.

C: Me, too.

T: Do you think there are other things about the rape itself that you haven't talked about that you want to be able to say something about?

This discussion has moved from a focus on her strengths to her decisions to disclose, which in this case are closely related. The expert companion entrusts to this rape survivor the choice about how much more to discuss the rape itself. This is different from the approach of many clinicians who treat trauma survivors who prescribe disclosure about the trauma as part of treatment. Here, the process is more collaborative. If the expert companion is going to highlight her strength, he will also need to collaborate with her as a partner in this therapy and share decision-making with her, especially about something as sensitive as the discussion of her rape.

C: I think I have said everything important about it. But I don't know. Is there something else you need to know?

T: I don't think I necessarily need to know a particular thing about the rape. I think I am most wanting to be sure that I am someone you can talk to openly about this, because I wouldn't want you to compromise our work together because it's embarrassing or feels emotionally unsafe, or something like that.

C: No, I'm OK.

This segment is a consideration of the strength of the therapeutic relationship and to what degree it can tolerate open self-disclosure. Julie's response that she's "OK" may sound a bit tepid, but the expert companion again has to determine how much to encourage openness and how much to respect the client's wishes. The question for the clinician, about needing to know more about it, indicates that work still needs to be done to establish this as a collaborative relationship. Here the client is putting too much decision-making power about disclosure into the hands of the clinician.

T: I trust you to know how much you need to talk about the rape. I ask questions mostly because I am thinking that there are things that are worth considering for you, not really because I need to know something. Of course, there are basic things that are important for me to understand, but the most important things I bring up are the things you may need to reflect on. But even here, it is not usually my call. You are aware of what you are trying to make sense of, or trying to decide. So, we are working on this together, but you can tell, I think, when you're talking about the things that are important for you.

The expert companion tries to outline the joint responsibilities for the therapy, that they are companions in this process, but that it is the client's journey more than the clinician's.

C: Yeah, but I haven't gone through anything like this before, so sometimes I'm not sure what I'm doing.
T: That's why you come so we can do it together.
C: Two heads are better than one!
T: Usually.
C: Although not when it comes to some of my friends. That's why I'm glad I came here. I sure have found out there are some people I thought would be a great help, but who were useless.
T: It's surprising. Sometimes in a bad way, sometimes in a good way, too?
C: Yeah, there have been a couple good surprises. Like my sister. We were OK with each other, I guess, but not terribly close. I always thought she saw me as the little sister who didn't have it together. This has changed things.
T: What has?
C: The rape!
T: Trick question—I'm thinking you really helped to change things.
C: What do you mean?
T: You told her about it, you trusted her with it.
C: OK, yeah, she couldn't have responded to me if I didn't tell her anything.
T: So, it's not the rape so much as what you did after.
C: Well, she was so supportive, and didn't start that critical stuff or anything.
T: Like you were to blame.
C: None of that. That was huge. It made me so much more comfortable. I was kind of waiting for it but it never came.
T: It sounds like she has really been great. Maybe partly because you gave her such a compliment by coming to her.
C: A compliment?
T: Yeah, trusting her with this was such a compliment.
C: She felt good because I trusted her.
T: That may have been huge for her.
C: Maybe so.
T: Brought you closer.

C: You know, I guess I have sort of been less open with her in the past few years. But I think it was because she was not too happy with some of what I was doing.

T: I'm glad that disclosing this to her has brought you closer.

C: Closer than we've ever been, I think. She'll call up a lot to check on me, and just hopping on that plane and coming down after it happened, well, that told me a lot.

T: Like what?

C: She loves me. (Begins to cry.)

T: Yes.

C: That sounds stupid.

T: Really?

C: I mean I guess I know my sister loves me, but it just, I don't know.

T: Made it clear that it's real love—she put it into action when she came and stayed with you.

C: Yes, I know it for sure. For sure.

T: You have been learning a lot about people in all this.

C: Oh, yes.

T: Who loves you and who doesn't.

C: Who to trust and who not to.

T: Who to talk to and who not to.

C: That's a lot.

T: Sure is. Pretty much the basics, don't you think?

C: The really important stuff.

This is clearly a discussion of disclosure, relationships, and PTG. It comes quite naturally in the course of conversation between a trauma survivor and an expert companion. But there are subtle ways that the clinician is ready to highlight certain aspects of the client's experience as opportunities appear to consider the gains that have come in the aftermath of trauma. However, at the same time, the negative aspects are not ignored. Instead, the conversation moves back and forth between the losses and the gains. In Julie's case, she has lost trust in a number of friends who have betrayed her in this difficult time in her life. Beyond that there may be a loss of a sense of innocence or a carefree approach to things. Perhaps that is what Julie's sister has been reacting to in the past, and has been unhappy with about Julie. Consider what happens next in this discussion that helps Julie understand better what has happened in her relationship with her sister, as a result of her being more open and accepting of her sister's concern and affection. Although the clinician is focusing on the change in her life that has come from all this, the client becomes reflective again about her relationship with her sister. The expert companion goes along with this train of thought and reflects along with her, resulting in a deeper, emotional understanding of her relationship with her sister, past and present.

T: Maybe this is stuff you haven't thought as much about before.

C: I think maybe I have been too busy having fun. Or what seemed like fun. I guess the fun is over.

T: This surely hasn't been fun.

C: Got that right. The worst time in my life.

T: This has changed a lot.

C: You know, my sister has always been the responsible one. I guess that's to be expected with her being four years older. She had to babysit for me and stuff, and we'd get into fights when she tried to boss me around. But she did all the right things my parents expected her to do. Go to college, get a good job, get married, have kids. She's really traditional, I guess. And here I am, having fun, partying, not too focused I guess you'd say. And she'd try to keep her mouth shut, I guess, but it would come out, like, Julie, what are you doing? And after Mom dies and then Dad had the stroke, she's taking care of him and I'm just keeping on like I had. Maybe she has every right to criticize me, she's taking on all the hard stuff. But she didn't. I guess I sort of anticipated she might say something like, "I told you so—see where it gets you living like that?" But she didn't, and you know, I think I need to thank her for that. I think I will.

T: What will you say?

C: Thanks for just loving me and not saying I told you so.

T: That would show a lot of appreciation.

C: I do appreciate that. She's such a giver, you know? Taking care of Dad, her kids, then coming down here for me. I guess I didn't appreciate it before, what she was doing.

T: Maybe you needed it more lately.

C: Maybe I needed it more before and didn't recognize it.

T: Maybe she was trying to find a way to love you more, but it wasn't working.

C: I wasn't ready for it.

T: Or maybe she couldn't figure out a way to show concern for you, without it coming out a little critical.

The clinician points out here that it is not so simple as her sister being giving and mature and Julie not. Julie collaborates here and she and her expert companion make sense out of the relationship these sisters have had. In doing so, Julie is not only learning about how her relationship with her sister has been changing, but also is creating a revised story of this relationship. We will discuss this process of narrative revision more in Chapter 7.

C: You know, after Mom died, and I was 16 she kind of started mothering me, and I don't think I liked it much.

T: I guess you weren't asking for it from her.

C: I sure wasn't. I started getting more wild then. She was probably worried about me. Maybe I am accepting a little of her mothering right now. Maybe that's why we're getting along. Maybe I need a mother right now.

T: It feels like mothering?

C: Well, I don't know about that. Maybe she's being my big sister who loves me. Hard to tell.

T: I guess it's just, love, one way or the other.

C: I love her, too.

T: I have a hunch that is not something you come out with much, with your sister.

C: I do now.

T: You say it.

C: Yes, and it's easy to say now.

T: These are big changes in your relationship.

C: Big changes in me. I am a different kind of sister, I guess. You know what's funny?

T: What's that?

C: I don't just talk with her about the rape. In fact, we don't really talk about the rape, after that first day she came down. We talk about other things. I talk with her about things I never talked with her about before.

T: That's what's different. It's not just about the rape, it's how you relate now.

C: That's true, we don't actually deal with the rape as much. More about what's happening now. I mean, a lot is related to the rape, but it's more than that.

T: So what do you talk about now?

C: What's going on with my friends. Ex-friends, sometimes. Oh, you know what's different? I just thought of this. Before my sister was like another Facebook friend. We'd go back and forth on that, but not really deep into anything, you know? But now we actually talk on the phone, and its more personal, just more personal.

T: I'm curious about something.

C: What's that?

T: How do you and your sister's conversations go? Do you get a sense its equal or does she tend to be one way and you are another? Is it still like she's the big sister and you are the younger? Or are the conversations actually different?

Here, the clinician is focusing on the specifics of the change that is reported by the client. Julie feels differently about her sister and their relationship, but now the question is how does this translate into behavior? Changes in the domain of PTG of Relationships with Others are often noticeable in changed behavior. It is useful to highlight these specific changes in order to consolidate them so that they are more likely to persist.

C: I guess we talk more as equals now—not totally but more so. We have such different lives, but we do talk more like I am not just some semi-screw up little sister.

T: You speak to her differently and she speaks to you differently?

C: Yes, I don't catch those little criticisms as much, I think. And maybe I'm not so defensive. I think I put that away when all this happened and I really needed her.

T: Both of you contribute to the changed relationship. You speak differently, with a different tone. Kinder tone with each other.

C: Yes.

T: And you talk about different things, not just the rape and what's happening in that case.

C: Yes, we talk about what I am going to do. Like I said, that old fun feels over for me, so we talk about what I'm going to do, the changes I'm going through.

T: It sounds like you are more open with her, you tell her more about what's going on inside you.

C: Definitely. Cause there's a lot going on, as you know.

T: So, are your conversations with her like ours?

C: Sort of, I do talk with about a lot of things we talk about. But not totally like our discussions. She tells me things, too.

T: About herself?

C: Yeah.

T: Is that different from before?

C: Yes, it is. She tells me more things that are going on, not just everyday stuff like what the kids are doing or something.

T: So, what kinds of things.

C: We talk about Dad, and not just how he's doing, but we actually talk about what it will be like when he dies and we have no parents left, and how that will feel. And how he's feeling about being so feeble and dependent. More about how we feel about things. And she tells me stuff about her husband Bobby that she never would talk about before.

T: She shares more things with you.

C: Yes, a lot more, it seems.

T: I wonder why that is.

C: I guess we've gotten more comfortable with each other.

Here, there is an opportunity to delve deeper into PTG. Clearly the relationship between Julie and her sister has changed. Julie can see that one aspect of this change involves their communication. She cites a number of ways they self-disclose much more than before, and how they are more comfortable in having this kind of conversation. But the clinician can help consolidate this change in the relationship further, by reflecting on other aspects that are not quite as evident or clearly labeled. Providing labels for these changes helps strengthen the cognitive access to them, aiding in their persistence, and perhaps further development, with even more intimacy in the relationship between these two sisters.

T: I am wondering how she sees you now. You say she doesn't treat you like a screw-up.

C: Maybe someone who just needs help.

T: But if that were the case the relationship wouldn't feel more equal, I would think.

C: Yeah, probably not.

T: So, there is probably something else going on. If she isn't seeing you so much as the somewhat mixed-up little sister, then what could it be?

C: I don't know. It's not like I've changed my life a lot in the past month. I still have the same stupid job and crummy apartment. I just have fewer crummy friends! And I'm sort of famous for being raped.

She says this humorously, which could be taken as a sign of not taking things seriously enough, or not taking things too seriously. This could be pursued in the conversation, but there is something that is the focus that is more important at the moment—her relationship with her sister that has shown indications of PTG.

T: It may have something to do with how you are handling all this. You went to the police. You risked your reputation and pretty much your social network by coming out with this. You knew it wouldn't be easy but you went forward anyway. And when bad things started to happen, you didn't flinch, you carried on. Maybe she sees all that.

C: She does, she knows all those things.

T: So, how would you think of someone who did that?

C: Pretty strong, I guess.

T: Your sister may see you as pretty strong.

C: Yes, I think so.

T: Another word comes to my mind, too. Respect.

C: You think she respects me? (She starts to cry again.)

T: What do you think?

C: I hope so. I guess I never thought she respected me.

T: That would be huge, too, wouldn't it.

C: Yes.

T: Does she speak to you more respectfully?

C: Yes.

T: That's what it sounds like, the way you described it.

C: She loves me and respects me.

T: I think so.

C: How could it change so fast?

T: Your relationship?

C: How she sees me.

T: She's probably always loved you, don't you think?

C: Yes, she just worried about me.

T: There's love in that.

C: Sure.

T: You were a bit frustrating, I suspect.

C: Oh yes, she'd agree with that!

T: The respect part, maybe that's new, I don't know. Do you think that she's always respected you in some way?

C: I don't know about that. Maybe that's new.

T: Because you are doing something very difficult. And maybe because you are willing to look at yourself and think that it is time to make some changes. That's hard, too. Maybe that's more to respect. Again, would you respect someone else who is doing what you are doing?

C: I think I would, yes. So, it's not so hard to believe my sister might respect me more now.

T: She must see you as someone who has enough sense for her to tell you about things that are important to her, things that are hard for her.

C: She is doing that.

T: She may have needed a sister, too, you know. Maybe it's good for her to have a grown-up sister.

C: What a way to grow up. Get raped.

T: That's not how you have grown up. You are growing yourself up through your choices in responding to this whole situation.

It is important to clarify to trauma survivors that it is not the trauma itself that is responsible for change, but how they respond to it. This not only gives credit and respect to the persons navigating these difficulties, but it is the truth. People choose their ways of responding.

C: Yeah, but sometimes I feel like I am just bumbling through.

T: It's hard to figure these things out, but you are sticking with it, and I think your sister respects that. I sure do.

Expert companions who accompany clients on their difficult journeys come to respect the people they work with enormously. So, this statement is not merely a therapeutic maneuver. But the clinician chooses to say this in order to let the client know that his hunches about her sister's view of her are based not only on the information that the client has shared about their conversations, but upon the clinician's own experience with the client.

C: Thank you, that means a lot to me. Because this is so hard.

T: And some other people are not giving you much respect.

C: Yes, that hurts.

T: That's part of why I respect you. You are willing to deal with that.

C: Thank you.

T: And that makes me think of how you are also dealing differently with other relationships as well.

C: Some people I have just written off.

T: That may have been wise in some cases.

This comment does not sound like resounding support for her decision to write some people off. It may be a mistake to support a complete rejection of some of her friends, since it is possible that some of these people may change their minds, and may apologize to her. It is only a month since the rape, and much may be in flux.

C: Yes, some people have really disappointed me and hurt me.

T: They certainly have. It's hard to know how to deal with that.

C: I've had no trouble telling some of them to go to hell.

T: I guess maybe not so hard in some cases.

C: The people I thought were really close to me, those are the hard ones. The ones who don't believe me.

T: The ones who have trouble believing Craig would do this.

C: Right.

T: Maybe it's more about that than not believing you.

C: But still, do they think I'd make this up?

T: That doesn't make any sense. What motive would they think you had for that?

C: I don't think they've come up with one that I remember.

T: Well, there are clearly the people who have been supportive and those who have not. Do the ones who have not been supportive know the real story? Did you actually tell them what happened?

C: No, a lot of them I'm not that close with. I wouldn't tell them all that stuff.

T: So, them not believing you is not as important, because they are not important enough to tell the story to.

C: I suppose that's true.

T: Are there any people you have shared the story with in some detail and who have not believed you?

C: Sharon and Connie.

T: Those hurt more.

C: Those are the worst for me.

T: So, what's up with them?

C: Well, Connie dates Craig's brother.

T: A loyalty problem there.

C: Yes, but we've been friends for about five years, so I don't really get it.

T: And Sharon? Why wouldn't she be supportive?

C: I can't figure it.

T: What has she said?

C: She just can't believe Craig would do that.

T: So what did you say to her?

C: Well, I just got so mad, I just walked out. I was at her apartment, telling her about it, and I just screamed at her that she was no friend at all, and I just walked out. Stormed out, really. I haven't talked to her since.

T: Has she tried to get up with you?

C: She texted me and said she couldn't believe I cussed her out and was so nasty to her. I didn't answer. She is worried that I was nasty to her and I was the one who was raped. She's not thinking of me at all.

Julie certainly has some way to go to have an understanding of how people who know both her and Craig might react to her accusations. The defensiveness she mentioned earlier in relation to her sister, is part of how she reacts in other relationships as well. So the changes being labeled as PTG do not represent a wholesale change in her personality. We might hope for more flexibility in her thinking, and empathy for others. Still, she shows an ability to protect herself from others who hurt her.

T: I remember you said earlier that you would have thought of yourself before dealing with the rape as a nice, kind person.
C: I guess I'm not too nice now.
T: Well, I was thinking that maybe it is good for you to be tougher with some people.
C: I think so. They just made me mad.
T: Because they hurt you. And are you concerned about how they may support Craig in other ways?
C: Like in court or something, like character witnesses?
T: Yes.
C: Yes, I do wonder what they would say. Like he's this great guy.
T: I also wonder if in addition to the two categories of people we are talking about there may be others.
C: Other categories. Like people who don't know what to think?
T: That might be one. Are there people like that?
C: I haven't taken a poll or anything.

This sarcastic comment may be an indication that the expert companion is losing his connection with Julie right here.

T: You can't go around trying to figure out what everybody thinks, because in the end, you just need to do the right thing.
C: That's right, I'm not going to let what people think get me off track.
T: That's that strength and toughness.

Here, the clinician works to get things back on track with Julie, realizing that she may take offense to his approach. It is best to heal therapeutic alliance ruptures as soon as possible.

C: That's what I have to have right now to get through this.
T: You'll have to figure out how you can be nice and kind while being tough as necessary, I guess.

C: I am having trouble doing both right now, so I'm going to have to be tough to get through this.

T: I hope some day Sharon changes her mind about this.

C: Well, if she doesn't, I'll just move on.

T: And if she does?

C: I guess it depends on when. I don't know, it just depends on when she comes around. At some point it may be too late.

The clinician explores whether Julie may be able to see the various possibilities in the various relationships she has, but she is not particularly capable of seeing these possibilities right now. So, it is time to let this be.

T: You've got a good sense right now of who is supportive, like your sister. People you can really talk openly with, and those who may be written off or put on the back burner. With all the strength you need to get through this, it may be best not to be distracted by them right now.

These are subtle suggestions that the future may allow something different in some of these relationships, but they are contained within an essential agreement with Julie that her focus right now is on self-protection. Her "toughness" is a strength she is coming to appreciate, and she has found of value, given that she was taken advantage of by someone she trusted. There are limits to change that must be accepted, especially so soon after a traumatic event. PTG can be highlighted when it is beginning to appear, but when the clinician is thinking that PTG may evolve at a later date, it is often better to let it be, and let the trauma survivor make these discoveries later.

This illustration includes much concern about disclosure and changes in relationships. There are concerns about disclosure to the police, to the therapist, to family, and to friends. At the same time it is clear she has invested in disclosure in therapy, and Julie tells the clinician that she trusts him. The recommendation from a trusted sister set the stage, but by being an expert companion, this possibility of trust was validated. In the kind of conversation that Julie can have with the clinician, exploration of various changes in relationships becomes a theme, as well as the personal strength that is emerging. It is clear that both these changes are still progressing, as she is figuring out how much to trust and disclose to others, and the important and sometimes subtle changes that happen in relationships when she risks self-disclosure, as she did with her sister. She has also learned the painful lessons of feelings of betrayal and abandonment when her disclosures are met with lack of trust by friends. Julie is also learning more about and how to be strong—does strength need to eschew empathy and charity when others misjudge, misunderstand, and disappoint her? These difficult considerations are clearly not possible for this client right now, and the expert companion knows when to let her be after making some probes to see if she is prepared for additional changes at this time.

seven
Creating a Narrative with Posttraumatic Growth Domains

A major and sometimes last element in PTG facilitation involves the creation of a narrative that incorporates the traumatic experiences and allows for the recognition of positive changes in the aftermath of the trauma. Narrative and constructivist approaches to therapy have become more appreciated in recent years, and represent a way to use the natural storytelling that is involved in all human interaction, including psychotherapy, to aid in healing (Neimeyer, 2006a, 2006b). By working on the narrative, the client comes to appreciate that there are various points of view from which events can be appreciated and understood. These perspectives represent opportunities to recast a traumatic event and its aftermath into constructive stories that can be used in the years ahead, forming a framework for a purposeful and satisfying life post-trauma. In facilitating PTG, it can be useful for the client to incorporate one or more of the five domains of growth into a life narrative, and to develop a robust set of core beliefs that will allow the trauma survivor to be able to be resilient to future challenges (Janoff-Bulman, 2006).

Although the focus of survivors is the story of the event and its aftermath, the narrative must also reflect the pre-trauma life as well. If we are to facilitate PTG, therapists must know what the client is changing *from*. The narrative is a complete life story, although certain aspects may be the focus. Certainly, one of the aspects of the life story that requires attention is the possibility that the client has suffered other major stressors prior to the one for which treatment is sought. Some clients may have had a lifetime of repeated traumatization, and treatment may need to focus on a series of events. The narrative may include how various events are related to each other, with each one playing a role in creating vulnerabilities and strengths in the client. The ability to link together events into a story that provides a sense of self has been termed *autobiographical reasoning* (Habermas & Bluck, 2000), and it is an important development during adolescence as identity is formed. This is the familiar concept developed by Erikson (1963). More recently McAdams (2006) has continued in this narrative tradition, and described how negative life events act as a catalyst for generativity in adulthood through *redemption sequences* that give meaning to suffering.

It is useful to encourage the process of narrative development by asking clients to create a simple timeline of their lives, locating both positive and negative events that they consider significant, so that they have a rough outline of a life narrative at the start of therapy. The clinician can then ask them to review the timeline, and in doing so, it can start to become clear how these various events are significant. Such a review may take a single session or several sessions of therapy. In the review of the life timeline, it often becomes apparent how difficult events have changed the direction of people's lives, changed their sense of identity, views of themselves, and of various core beliefs. Clinicians can ask questions to make these changes become clearer to the client, since the person reporting these events may not have considered all their effects. These questions include, "How did going through this change you?" or "How do you think your life might have been different if this hadn't have happened?" or "How did your life change direction after this?" It will be important to listen for indications of PTG in these reports, as well as healthy coping and new core beliefs.

The revision of the life narrative that can happen in the aftermath of tragedy is co-authored by the trauma survivor and the expert companion. The survivor benefits from expert companionship in narrative construction because it is hard to appreciate oneself only from an internal point of view. The expert companion notices things the trauma survivor may miss. For example, one of the basic questions the clinician may ask, is "Given how horrible this event was, is there any possibility of anything valuable coming from it?" The clinician may also say "I notice some things that you tend to overlook in yourself."

Trauma survivors are prone to focus on the horror of what they went through, how it has hurt or damaged them, and what they have lost. They are often unsure of how to get through their trials, if they will ever heal, and how much discomfort they will need to endure along the way. The narrative must include all aspects of the client's experience, because growth does not come from denial, but from confronting the existential questions raised, and from sharing these experiences with appropriate others. By considering the entire narrative, survivors of traumatic events become trauma experts, knowledgeable about the details and nuances of trauma. They also may uncover aspects of themselves that would not have been evident otherwise.

As the narrative is reviewed and perhaps revised, it can become apparent that there have been various eras in a person's life, and perhaps various identities as well. Generally, people manage trauma better when they can recognize that there are different aspects to their identity and when one is weak or threatened, another remains intact (Showers & Ryff, 1996). People often become trauma experts when they struggle to find their way despite the advice of others. For example, grieving people who are told by others that they must "move on" discover that engaging the grief may be a better way for them, even though it can feel so painful that they wish they could simply, move on. Often the job of the expert companion is to support the instinctual moves of trauma survivors, helping them see what is right about their perceptions and choices and how much they can count on their own strengths. When the story is told, it may be one where the client is able to see themselves as more assertive and confident. Sometimes it is more difficult for clients to notice the positive aspects of their experiences, and there may need to be more direct methods utilized to help them notice. These methods may involve diaries or self-monitoring tasks similar to those employed in the "well-being therapy" described by Fava (Fava, 1996; Fava & Ruini, 2003).

Sometimes the themes of growth in the survivor's story are so subtle that the expert companion needs to point them out. This is especially true for clients whose identity involved a sense of invulnerability or great strength. Clients who were like this may desperately wish to return to their former selves, and they may have trouble appreciating the paradox of vulnerability and strength—that people can get stronger by confronting weakness. One client who went through difficult chemotherapy for cancer felt guilty about talking to her husband about it, feeling like she was a complainer, even though he was very supportive. The clinician allowed her to show her vulnerability by suggesting that she could talk all she wanted as long as she did not *whine*. She had something to avoid, whining, while the rest of the talk became all right with her. Integrating the sense of vulnerability into the life narrative is a characteristic of almost all clinical work with survivors of major life crises. But PTG can involve an appreciation of how acknowledging vulnerability is a subtle strength. In the aftermath of major stressors, many people can feel like weaklings or failures because they were not able to prevent the tragic circumstances, they are not able to reverse them, their emotions overwhelm them at times, and they have trouble figuring out how to proceed. In the face of all this, subtle strength is endurance, acceptance, expressiveness and support-seeking—tendencies that may have previously been seen only as vulnerabilities.

In a narrative constructivist approach, clinicians help trauma clients shift the schemas that are used to define identity, and in particular what it means to be strong. Those who see themselves as vulnerable may be helped to see that survivor status connotes strength. However, it is important not to reconstrue everything as strength. Vulnerability is real, and trauma forces people to face this difficult truth. A clear-eyed vulnerability requires existential courage to live in the face of death (Maddi, 2012). The new life narrative that incorporates this truth may enable the trauma survivor to face their ultimate and inescapable life task, death, more gracefully.

In the following case example, we meet Mitchell, a 55-year-old man who had a stroke one year ago. He went through successful rehabilitation, but post-stroke brain scans showed an inoperable aneurysm that could kill him at any moment.

He has been forced to cease any activity that might raise his blood pressure or heart rate. He is fully disabled and stays at home most of the day except for short drives to do errands. His teenage children and his wife all lead busy lives, but he cannot. The following excerpts are from session after Mitchell had been in psychotherapy for two months.

T: We've been speaking of how to find meaningful activity for yourself. How have you been doing with that lately?

C: Not great. I've always been physically active, going to the gym, playing basketball. I'm not used to sitting around.

T: What have you considered?

C: I've been trying to stay away from the TV, I don't think that would be good for me. I've tried a little gardening, as long as it isn't too strenuous. But it all feels like just trying to fill time. What a way to live.

T: You don't know how much time you have to fill.

C: Why start something you might not finish.

T: This whole approach to living is completely contrary to what you used to do.

C: I would just do whatever I wanted. Work hard, play hard. I've always been in good shape and never felt my age, as it were. Oh, I've lost a step maybe in the past few years, but nothing that made too much difference. Life has always been pretty good. My wife and I were planning on doing all kinds of traveling after the kids grew up, and especially when we retired. Now I feel tethered to the hospital. And I'm just living minimally. Just barely living.

T: In terms of doing, it certainly must feel that way. From all that activity, down to idle. Like a fast car that's only got first gear.

Here the clinician makes a subtle comment in order to set up further discussion. He agrees with the client that his activity level is very reduced, and this feels like hardly living, but says that "in terms of doing, it certainly must feel that way."

C: That's me for the rest of my life, such as it is.

T: I wonder if you ever thought you'd be in such a position.

C: Not until I was 90.

T: It's like being 90.

C: Actually it's not. If I were 90, I would probably be slow, or in pain, or have lost my memory, or something, and I don't have any of those problems. I'm just a healthy guy who may die any minute.

T: Or live another two or three decades.

C: Who knows?

T: In some ways you are no different from many people who feel healthy.

C: Anyone can die any minute, is what you are saying.

T: Right. Maybe a person doesn't realize they have some physical problem that would kill them. Or they get hit by the proverbial bus.

C: Yeah, but I *know* I have the problem.

T: That is different. And knowing this you have altered your entire lifestyle.

C: Sometimes I've thought, maybe I should just live normally and take my chances, but then I think of Carla and the kids, and I think they want me around. Even in my state.

T: I would think they do.

C: Thank goodness we don't have financial problems.

T: You set them up pretty well there.

C: So, I still haven't figured out how to do this, even though I've known for a year. You know, once the rehab was over, I got I little lost. The rehab gave me something to do, to concentrate on. A little job, you know. That was my job—speech therapy, OT, and so forth. Now, it's up to me.

T: To structure your day.

C: I haven't done much with that.

T: But also to figure out what to do with your life.

C: It all sure has changed.

It is clear that Mitchell is confronted with more than the practical concern about what to do during the day. The bigger question is—what is the purpose for his life, because it has been stripped down to very few possibilities. The stark change in his life course presents an opportunity to describe the life narrative, including past, present and future. But the future is very murky. As the life narrative is described, *the work of the clinician as expert companion is to facilitate the consideration of PTG that is already occurring or that which may still be possible.*

T: Your life is like one of those before and after pictures.

C: Right. Here's Mitchell before his stroke, a healthy, active happy guy. Here's Mitchell after his stroke. A slug.

T: You know in the before and after pictures, the after one is usually the improvement.

C: That's true. So this must be a bad analogy.

T: Maybe not totally.

C: You know, that's really true. You know I'm still kind of mad about all this, and I come in and complain and stuff, but actually I don't feel as bad about it as I used to. I'm starting to figure a few things out.

T: I'm curious what they are.

C: I think I've been reluctant to talk about it, because in a way I don't want to stop being mad. I don't want to accept this. But I'm accepting it. But I don't want to give up or give in, I guess. If I just accept this is the way it's going to be, it feels like giving in. I've never been a quitter.

T: That would feel like being a quitter.

C: Quitting my old life or the possibility of it. That's kind of stupid though, because I know it's over. So, I'm not really quitting, it just feels that way. So, I've got all this confusion inside.

T: Accepting, but being mad, trying to figure out how not to be a quitter.

C: Yeah, just a lot of mixed up stuff.

T: So what happens when you are finding yourself accepting?

C: I'm not as mad, I feel calmer. So that's good. I don't want to kill myself by getting mad I'm going to die—that would be crazy, don't you think.

T: Sounds kind of crazy, doesn't it? A little funny.

C: Yeah, a little funny. Sometimes I think this is funny. It should be a comedy routine or some kind of movie. "The guy who could die any minute."

T: It sure is a new way to try to live. Very different. It kind of reminds me of the difference between us and animals, supposedly. We are the ones with the self-awareness that we will die someday. Animals seem blissfully ignorant of it. You have it at a whole other level, this realization.

C: So I'm even less animal, I guess.

T: Maybe even more human—how's that strike you?

C: Wow, that's something isn't it. More human, because I am more aware. So the more death stares you in the face, the more human you are.

T: Maybe the less you fool yourself, or the less you just go through the routine without thinking about how you are living your life.

C: Yeah, I used to just go through the routine every day. Get up, go to work, not even think about it. That was my old life, treating it like I was going to live forever. Fooling myself like that, like I had all the time in the world. Now this part of my life is so different. I get up, thinking, what should I do today? I just haven't had many answers.

T: Those are the little immediate, day-to-day answers. But it sounds like you are getting the bigger answers, starting to. About how to see this whole thing, accept it.

C: Starting to. You know the breathing exercise for my anxiety? I sure have time to do that, so I do it twice a day, sometimes more. I'm feeling a lot calmer. And since I don't have any deadlines to speak of, I move slower, and that's not a bad thing, I'm finding out. I'm calmer, slower, move at a slower pace. It's like I consider things rather than doing them automatically.

Perhaps what Mitchell is talking about here is the PTG domain of New Possibilities. The old possibilities have had to be set aside, and he is forced to deal with what is left and make the most of it. Having been forced by circumstance to do so, he is beginning to discover possible advantages of this new way.

T: So, compared to life before the stroke, you have a new way of moving through the day. More reflectively and deliberately. And you do your breathing, too.

C: Yeah, that's it.

T: It sounds sort of like a meditation. A moving around, awareness meditation. Living life more like you are in a meditation.

C: Sounds kind of weird. But that's pretty much what I am doing. But what is the point of that?

T: The point for you?

C: And others. Like my family, what good does it do for them?

T: What are you like for them to be around these days.

C: Well, I am around, which is a big change from the way it was when I was working. I used to get a lot of overtime, and I always took it, so I wasn't around a lot of evenings and even some weekends. So, that's something that's better. And I'm not stressed out, because I'm not busy with anything, and I'm doing my breathing, and that anxiety has really calmed down. I get a little when I start thinking of dying, but I am doing better with letting that go—you know, letting it drift over into my periphery like we said, rather than having it smack in front of me. So, I am calmer to be around, and I have plenty of time to listen. I am listening really good now—what else do I have to do?

T: I'll bet your kids like that.

C: Yeah, but they're teenagers, so they don't talk that much anyway. But when they do, they have my full attention. I'm thinking, maybe this is one of the last times they will get to talk to me, I'd better make it good! Sounds a little morbid, but it's a good motivator.

T: It sounds like death has gone from being really scary to being motivating, so you live a little better. More conscious of what's at stake.

C: That's right, that's what's happening. So, I have a whole new way of living life in terms of knowing what's at stake, but I can't figure out what to do with all this time. It's good to have plenty, so I am not rushed and stressed, but I should be doing something with it all. I really see time as precious now. I don't want to waste it.

T: So, you can see clearly what you were like before the stroke, active, a bit ambitious, acting like you had all the time in the world. Happily oblivious.

C: You got it.

T: And since the stroke, knowing what your body could do to you, you are more aware of the precious time you have, without knowing how much. And you're moving from being mad and anxious about this to being accepting and calm. We don't know yet how you will be using this time in the most constructive way. But that seems to be the next phase.

C: I am thinking about doing things I might like, but then I think that might be selfish, so I think of how I should help out other people.

T: You are helping out your kids.

C: Yeah, a better father, even if I can't play ball with them.

T: But you mean people outside your family?

C: I don't know. I've got plenty of family.

T: You haven't mentioned your wife.

C: Oh, I've been cooking so she has supper when she gets home from work. I do the grocery shopping, clean the house up. She loves it. She says this actually works better for her. She likes having a wife.

T: Is that satisfying for you?

C: I like pleasing her. It's not the most exciting thing.

T: That doesn't sound like you are a slug like you said.

C: Nah, not really, but I just mean compared to before. I don't work, don't do the outside like the lawn and stuff. Jimmy's picked up the slack on that.

T: So let me see what we have. You are much more reflective about your life, rather than just hurriedly going through the motions. You take time for your relationships with family. You recognize the importance of using your time well, and want to do something for other people, not just indulge yourself in something mindless like TV. You are a different sort of fellow. And still in process. I wonder what we'll be seeing down the line.

These last remarks by the clinician provide a summary of various aspects of posttraumatic growth, reflecting the client's own reports. The clinician does not explicitly say that the client has grown because of having to deal with the change in his physical condition, but that is clearly implied. *The clinician does not have to prove that PTG is in the story of the present, or recite the five statistical domains of PTG. Instead, the clinician reflects on the specifics that this client describes himself.* The clinician also points to the next chapters in the story by saying something about what might happen next. For a man who often thinks about his own death, this is likely to be encouraging. His psychotherapist thinks of him as a man with a future.

C: Yeah, I'm not doing too bad.

T: Especially under the circumstances that would rattle most anybody. I don't think you have recognized these changes, positive changes, clearly enough until we start talking about them.

C: No, I haven't put it all together like that.

T: I also think that despite the huge change in your life, the old you is still here, too.

C: Yeah, I'm still me.

T: How so?

C: We'll, I've always been pretty easy going, and I'm still that way, now that the anxiety has eased up. I like to have fun, and I still do. Just can't play like I used to. I've always been pretty simple—didn't need a lot to be happy.

T: That all helps in this situation, I think. Easy going, pretty happy, not needing a lot. That fits with what's going on now.

C: Yeah, I'm still me, just version Two. I guess I'm a little better in some ways. I hope I have a lot of time to live like this. It's not too bad, and maybe I'm easier to live with.

The client himself can also see the positive changes, and in noticing them, there is a glimmer of a more purposeful, meaningful life.

T: And you also wonder about how much time you have, thinking of dying. That gets some anxiety going.

C: But I'm getting better at moving it aside. I've learned that one pretty well, you know, instead of having the big battle with it.

T: Good, I am glad you're applying that. It gets easier with practice.

Here the client is referring to the mindfulness practice of letting go of the struggle with what makes people anxious and various ruminations. As we saw in the discussion of emotional regulation, it has been important for him to be able to address his anxiety with a breathing exercise and the mindfulness practice of letting disturbing thoughts move to the periphery rather than being confronted directly.

C: I really do appreciate life more. I go out into the yard and look around, and I see things I would usually overlook. I'm much more observant. Even when I go to the grocery store, I'm taking my time, looking around, watching people, looking at stuff.
T: Savoring the grocery store.
C: Crazy, huh? But that's just what I'm doing. There's a lot of simple stuff to savor.
T: You didn't make time for that before.
C: I've got plenty now.
T: Because you're not working. But on the other hand, you feel like you don't have much.
C: Yeah, that's funny isn't it. I feel like I have all this time, because I may not have much time. I sure am glad I'm not working, when I think about it.
T: It's like being retired.
C: Prematurely. But I had been planning on retiring at 62. So, I'm only seven years short.
T: So, if you think of yourself as being retired, how does that feel?
C: Not bad, really.
T: If you had gotten yourself financially in the spot to retire at 55, would you have done it?
C: Yes, sir. So this is like early retirement. I can see that. The problem is I can't do some of the things I was looking forward to.
T: That's the bad part.
C: Along with maybe dying of course.
T: Of course.
C: But, like you said, it could be a long time.
T: Do you wish to think of it like a long time or a short time?
C: Hmmm. I've been thinking short, but it could be long. Longish, maybe.
T: Maybe both short and long, like we were saying. If you think short, you savor things. If you think long, you invest more, and see the value of starting things.
C: How do you do both at once?
T: Thinking both ways at once. That takes some practice, too. Have you ever seen those visual illusions, you look at something one way, and then it switches into another figure?
C: Yeah, it's kind of like that, isn't it? Both at once, but you have trouble actually seeing them together.

T: You never had to think about this stuff before, did you?

C: Never did. Now I look back and it's quite a story isn't it, and this is a pretty interesting part. Different from most people.

T: You are living a pretty unique life in some ways.

C: I guess I should appreciate parts of it.

T: Some parts are worth appreciating.

C: I can see that.

This client is coming to appreciate the interest and value of his own story. Earlier he asked what good were his changes to other people. There is now another opportunity to explore this question, given that he is recognizing the value of his changed life.

T: You mentioned earlier that you weren't sure of the value of these changes to other people, and we talked about how you treat your kids and your wife better. I wonder if there is even more value for them, and there could be this value for other people, too. You see life from a different perspective, you know, not going through the motions as if you have all the time in the world. That is a valuable thing, and maybe your family sees that.

C: They might see I've changed like that.

T: Do you think?

C: We don't really talk about deep things like that.

T: They might see it anyway.

C: Maybe, I don't know.

T: What if you said some of these things out loud?

C: They'd think old dad had lost it.

T: Or maybe they would listen.

C: So, what should I say?

This is very dangerous territory, where expert companionship is important. Clinicians should be careful about telling their clients what to say or do in situations like this. They should be respectful and help clients find their own way and their own voice. In doing so clients may find themselves acting out the hero's journey reflected in ancient myths. After doing battle against great odds, the hero returns home with new ways of living to share with those who did not go on the quest. These new ways of living should incorporate core beliefs that can support people through further difficulties. However, it is hard for most trauma survivors to perceive the heroic aspect of their experiences and the expert companion might help them reconceive the concept of the hero (Birkett, 2011).

T: I don't know explicitly. But you have been saying to me things that sound pretty important.

C: I don't say much about what I'm thinking or what I'm going through.

T: Maybe your family is interested but is worried about bringing things up.

C: So, I should gather them around and tell them what's going on?

This sounds a little sarcastic, and it is clear this client is not comfortable with the idea of disclosing about his changes, or talking about his own experiences. So, the warning has been issued to treat this subject carefully with him, and remember not to forget expert companionship in this process.

> T: I'm just thinking that you have gifts to bring. That this experience with life, and death, has brought to you new perspectives that you need not keep all to yourself. You have been starting to see them as valuable. The things like living life more deliberately and at a pace where you can observe things and appreciate things, including listening in a more focused and attentive way. I'm just thinking that you are a pretty generous man, one who doesn't keep everything for himself, and you might wish to share these gifts.
> C: My wife always bought the kids gifts.
> T: These are gifts of a different kind.
> C: Sure are.

Instead a hammering away at this, the concept of the gifts he has to bring, the clinician guesses that given his focus on dying, he might have been thinking about his legacy. This is a common concern for American adults in mid-life, and finding an expression of this "redemptive self" (McAdams, 2012) provides a pathway to a meaningful life story and everyday action.

> T: Have you thought at all about how you will be remembered?
> C: Yeah, with dying on my mind, that's one of the things.
> T: So, what have you thought?
> C: I'd like to be remembered, sure. I've thought a bit of what they'll say about me when I'm gone.
> T: So, this is of some importance to you.
> C: I guess I'd like to think I mattered.

The client says he wants to have mattered, perhaps in the sense that others have benefited from his presence. This is important to him, and therefore useful to explore. However, the exploration of this is not so much a way to make sure he leaves a legacy, but to help him determine how he wants to live now. The legacy is the byproduct of a well-lived life. Here we see that the focus is not exclusively on alleviating or relieving symptoms, but on helping the client build a life with even more satisfaction and sense of purpose than before. With a new sense of purpose, the trials that trauma survivors endure can become something meaningful as well, not merely pain to be endured. The purposes that guide their post-trauma living allow them to endure other possible stresses and traumas. They develop resilience through construction of new core beliefs that sustain them in the face of such difficulties, as opposed to the old beliefs that did not provide enough support. Their lives can become models for others, while the trauma survivors are living, and after they have died.

T: So what will they say?

C: He was a fun-loving good guy, who also worked hard, didn't complain when he got a raw deal.

T: OK, that encompasses the way you've lived up until now. How about the rest? Will they simply see you as uncomplaining?

C: There's more to it than that.

T: From what you've been saying.

C: It's hard to put into words.

Many clients coping with major stressors may never have explicitly articulated precisely what their core beliefs are. People's basic philosophy of living may often remained unexplored until they are forced by events that may have life and death implications. The expert companion must be patient to help clients with this articulation, so that their beliefs do not sound like mere clichés and meaningless platitudes.

T: Let's see if we can figure this out—the things that really make sense to you now as a good and right basis for living.

C: A lot of it is like a feeling of what's right but I don't know how to say it. Some of it I guess I've always known, but know better now. I don't just know it, I *know* it.

This explanation from the client reflects the difference in the experience of the core beliefs in the aftermath of trauma; they may have a strong emotional element and are not mere intellectual musings. Consider how Mitchell works on describing his beliefs, and what the expert companion does to help.

T: Like knowing it in your bones.

C: It's the difference between hearing about things, or thinking about them, and being so convinced you just go with them.

T: Live them.

C: Right, live them. Like I always thought, like most people do, I guess, that you are supposed to put family first, beyond work, but now I really do.

T: But what if you still could work? Someone might say, "What would he do if he could still work like before, I'll bet he would."

Here is a gentle challenge to the loyalty to this core belief. The client is saying that he is more convinced of it and is willing to stake major life decisions on it. This challenge in some ways reflects the distrust some researchers have of reports of PTG by survivors of highly stressful events (Gunty, Frazier, Tennen, Tomich, Tashiro, & Park, 2010; Hobfoll, Hall, Canetti-Nisim, Galea, Johnson, & Palmieri, 2007). To what degree do trauma survivors translate their thoughts and new perspectives into lasting noticeable change? As clinicians, we wish to see such change, so it is good to discuss the specifics of the client's commitments.

C: Knowing what I do now, I wouldn't work like I used to, overtime and all of that. I'd try to be more normal about it. I'd take vacations. You know, I used to leave vacation time on the table almost every year. It doesn't roll over until the next year, so every year I would lose a few days—sometimes a week or two! Now I think that's crazy, but before, I was trying to get as much money in the bank as possible.

T: You don't see that as so important anymore? You do have money that is helping out now.

C: I lost a lot of time, though.

T: Time and money are both needing to be budgeted, aren't they?

C: We don't have unlimited amounts of either, do we?

T: No, but most people only think of budgeting their money, not their time.

C: And like I was saying before, time is precious to me now, so I don't want to waste it. I'm not sure how much is in the bank.

T: What other things do you really know now? Things you are willing to actually live by?

C: Like I said, my relationships. I take my time with people. I guess that's a time thing, too, huh?

T: Like you mentioned listening to your kids.

C: Yeah, but you know what? Not just them, but other people as well. Like people I just see in stores and whatnot. I just chat with them, not just do my business and leave. You know I was just thinking I'm like those old people who can aggravate other people by just taking their time, chatting, and gumming up the whole works. I remember at the store, some of those people I would just try to move on 'cause I had things to do. Now it's like I'm one of them.

T: Retired, relaxed, with time on your hands.

C: Yeah, but also thinking that these little things are important.

T: I guess you think more like an older person now?

C: Maybe so.

T: Like your situation is more like an older person's?

C: Yeah, except like I said the body still works like before, except for that one problem.

T: Your perspective has changed from a middle-aged guy trying to store away as much as possible, to an older man who is savoring the life he has left.

C: That's what's happening.

As a clinician is involved with conversations such as this, it is useful to bring to mind various concepts that relate to what the client is expressing. Here, we see elements of Erikson's (1963) ideas about wisdom in late life, and existential themes (Frankl, 1963). This discussion about *mortal time*, described by McQuellon and Cowan (2010) as an acute recognition of one's mortality, is richest when people are facing life threats.

T: I'm thinking these are perspectives that can carry you throughout your life.

C: I've really learned what's important.

T: Do you think you are still learning?

C: I think so, because I actually think about this stuff quite a bit.

T: I'm wondering about another thing—your view of yourself. You've been through a lot.

C: Like I'm old, like the old people?

T: No, I was thinking about how much you appreciate the strength it takes to go through something like this.

C: You know, sometimes people have said to me, like in rehab, how strong I must be to get through this. But, what am I supposed to do? Give up?

T: You're not a quitter.

C: Right, but I have to just keep going.

T: You said you decided against suicide.

C: When you are just trying to survive you do it. What special strength is in that? Who wouldn't?

This comment by the client is one that becomes familiar when working with many trauma survivors. Others may see them as strong, but many of these survivors they see themselves as merely doing what needs to be done. Trauma survivors who view themselves this way are showing good coping and resilience, but they may benefit from also appreciating more this strength in themselves.

T: So you don't think that you are any stronger than you might have thought you were before all this happened.

C: Maybe some. It has been a challenge, and still is. It's a different kind of strength, I guess. Maybe that's it, stronger in certain ways. A weird kind of strength.

T: Where you can't just roll over your problems or vulnerabilities.

C: Right, I have to carefully figure out how to live like this. I used to just figure I could barrel through things before.

T: You have this real, physical vulnerability that limits you, that you have to be careful about, yet you have also been able to face the possibility of death remarkably well. You are coping with the anxiety successfully now, and you haven't really gotten depressed about it. You haven't been lying in bed crying, or drinking yourself in to oblivion, or any of those kinds of things people sometimes do. I know you said you did think of killing yourself, but it sounds like this was never a serious possibility for you.

C: I'm just not the kind of person for that stuff. I've always done things, I'm not going to take it lying down, you know?

T: So it's not surprising you've been coping this well.

C: Sometimes I didn't think I really was coping so well. When I was getting so panicky and all.

T: How do you see it now?

C: I am feeling pretty good about how I'm doing. A lot of people would freak out, I'll bet. I want to show my kids I'm OK, too. I'm doing it, I'm good.

This discussion highlights the PTG domain of Personal Strength, that this client describes, at least to some degree. The clinician explores this possibility and lets the client define it his way. However, the client has not yet indicated he has experienced changes in other common domains of growth including new possibilities and spiritual or religious changes. The clinician explores these in a straightforward, but gentle way.

> T: We've been talking about the degree to which going through this has enhanced your appreciation for living life, as you have slowed things down, observed and savored your experiences, how you have taken more time to attend to your relationships with others, and how you have redefined what it means to be strong. I am also thinking that you may be spending your time differently, focusing on different things. Like the gardening you have been doing.
> C: That's one thing I still don't have a handle on. I'm experimenting there. You know, I'm going back to things I had let go of. They may sound kind of silly, but I'm getting some enjoyment. When I was a kid, I really enjoyed stamp collecting. Me and my dad used to do it together. I found the old stamp albums in the attic and they were in OK shape and I've been looking them over and looking up stamps online. It's been fun. Brings back good memories, and I enjoy studying and learning things. So, I've been starting, doing that a little bit.
> T: Good for you. Lots of good things about that—memories, learning, fun.
> C: I am thinking about getting some more stamps—I'm not sure if I should start to invest in all this again, but it's really not that expensive.
> T: You can try it out and see how it goes—it's up to you. But things like this are good—some intellectual exercises.

New Possibilities may be minimal here, but the expert companion is gently encouraging the client to explore them, and trusting of Mitchell to find his own way with them. This kind of exchange would not be possible, or desirable, if the clinician had not established an empathic alliance with the client. An alliance that included not only the mutually respectful relationship between an expert and a client, but also the relationship between two equals going together on a long journey.

> T: I find myself wondering as well about whether having to deal with this life and death situation has prompted any consideration of spiritual or religious matters.
> C: I've been thinking about dying more and how it will happen. It may be so quick I won't even know what happened, or it may be messy. I guess we'll have to see. But mostly I just try to put it out of my mind. I've never been religious or anything, and in my mind death and religion seem to go together in some way, I don't know, just about heaven and all. I guess I believe in heaven, sort of, but not totally. I just figure it will be heaven or nothing. I don't get into it

much, because that kind of stuff has raised my anxiety, and I don't need that. I just figure, focus on what's going on now, take care of business now. I can't do anything about the heaven stuff. Either it's there or not.

T: Not much different from how you've always thought about this?

C: No, not really. I'm the same guy that way. I just try to take care of business, and leave the stuff I know nothing about to someone else.

Mitchell's experience includes some aspects of PTG, but not others. If he were to complete the PTGI (Tedeschi & Calhoun, 1996), he might report high levels of growth in Appreciation of Life, Relating to Others, moderate levels on Personal Strength, and low levels on new Possibilities and Spiritual Change. It is important for clinicians to remember that each client is likely to have a different pattern of PTG—including the complete absence of any form of posttraumatic growth. Clinicians also need to remember that clients tend to focus on what is true for them in the here and now. PTG can change over time, although we have only a few longitudinal studies to go on (Dekel, Ein-Dor, & Solomon, 2012; Schroevers, Helgeson, Sandernnan, & Ranchor, 2010; Wolchik, Coxe, Tein, Sandler, & Ayers, 2009).

T: This is an ongoing process of change you are in, but I get the impression that you are clear that you have changed, and mostly in positive ways, although your life situation itself is mostly negative. That's an important distinction—the situation versus you. The situation is mostly worse...

C: Except for having the time off, or retired, or whatever we want to call it.

This kind of distinction, between the stressful situation on the one hand, and the person's experience and stance toward the situation, on the other, their experience is crucial for trauma survivors who experience PTG. Mitchell's situation is not better. But, as a person, he might be different in a very positive way. It can be useful for clinicians to help trauma survivors recognize both the positive and the negative aspects of their lives. We must not ask them to be Pollyannas about their losses and tragedies. Expert companions empathetically acknowledge the bitter parts of the client's life; with people who are suffering, there is no choice. Expert companions help clients accept both the reality of their suffering and the possibilities for growth that such suffering may allow.

T: Right, but would you agree that *you* are mostly better?

C: Yes, more and more, now that I am adjusting to it and not so anxious. I can see the before and after, too like you say, the whole story of it.

T: You have a pretty amazing life, Mitchell.

C: I guess I do, although I'm not sure people would want to trade me for it. Well, then again, maybe some would.

T: If this were some kind of strange game show and you could trade your life for someone else's, blind, not knowing what you were getting, would you do it?

C: Wow, I'm not sure. At the beginning of this I think I would have said yes, but now, I don't know, I think I might stick with mine. Man, that really is something. That I can be thinking that way. Wow.

T: Maybe it's because you are finding that the way you are living…

C: It's more a way to get the most out of the life I've got. Maybe I don't have as much of a life, but I'm getting more out of what I have.

By saying this, Mitchell is recognizing PTG and how it may fit into his evolving life narrative. He has a perspective on how to live, a perspective that allows him to appreciate the life he is living. This perspective, and the core beliefs that comprise it, may be hard for him to articulate at times, but he has a visceral and intuitive sense of it being right. The heroic victories of the survival after trauma tend to yield the emotional as well as the intellectual appreciation of the well-lived life, and what is learned in this highly emotional experience may well endure.

eight
Existential, Religious, and Spiritual Growth

There currently is a significant degree of scholarly interest in the relevance of religion and spirituality to psychological functioning. But there is no clear consensus on the meaning of these two concepts. As we use the terms, these concepts have overlapping but somewhat different meanings. *Religion* describes a system of "belief, values, and practices" (Mahrer 1996, p. 435) that are organized around beliefs about God or a similar kind of transcendent force. Being "religious" implies having a belief in the existence of God, or similar entities, but it does not necessarily mean affiliation with a particular religion or religious group. *Spirituality*, on the other hand, describes a less specific set of beliefs or experiences, and the word currently tends to connote subjective experiences that have in common a connection to something transcendent, or at least an existential state beyond the self (Hill & Pargament, 2008).

In some ways, the typical psychotherapist and the average citizen are in different religious cultures. This is certainly the case in the United States. The vast majority of Americans believe in God and describe themselves as religious. However, some of the major figures in the history of psychotherapy, for example, Sigmund Freud and Albert Ellis, held quite negative views of religion and of religious beliefs. Surveys of mental health workers show that mental health professionals tend to be less religious in all aspects of religious life, including beliefs, attendance, and practice. A poll of American psychologists indicated that about 32 percent believed in God (Delaney, Miller, & Bisono, 2007); this represents a great disparity from the general public, with more than 90 percent reporting a belief in God (Gallup, June 3, 2011). In addition, mental health professionals are much more likely to say that they once did believe in God, but they no longer do, a change in views that is much less common in the general population (Delaney, *et al.*, 2007). Since clinicians who are religious may be more likely to respond to surveys about religion and spirituality (Shafranske & Malony, 1990), there may be quite a gulf between the views of psychotherapists and the views of the people who become their clients.

Despite this rather large religious divide between clinicians and the general public, the views that psychotherapists have of the spiritual and religious beliefs of their clients tends to be one of acceptance. The spiritual dimension of life is viewed as important by a significant proportion of North American psychologists, and interest in religion and spirituality among researchers and practitioners has grown in the last 20 years (Hill & Pargament, 2008). This benevolent view is desirable, because posttraumatic growth may be evidenced in the broad areas of spirituality, religion, and existential belief and experience. In this chapter, after a case (Shanneesha) is presented, the chapter will describe the following: existential issues in the aftermath of trauma, spirituality and religion in the aftermath of trauma, and posttraumatic growth and spirituality in treatment. The chapter will end with brief discussion of the different kinds of orientations clinicians may have to their clients' religious and spiritual assumptions.

Shanneesha

Shanneesha was a 22-year-old college senior, majoring in marketing, and she was engaged to be married. During her sophomore year, her friend Sherry had died in an accident. Although she grieved the loss of her friend, she had managed to be resilient in the face of her loss. In her previous year in college she became engaged. She had known her fiancé, DeShawn, for three years and she knew that they shared common interests in sports, movies, live theater, and music, and that their core values were the same. They were both committed members of a nondenominational Christian church and regarded their religious beliefs as the main guide for how they should live. They both wanted careers, but they also planned to have children after being married for two or three years, and they wanted to share parental responsibilities. Their futures were bright, and as Shanneesha joked with one of her friends, quoting an old popular song, "our future is so bright we have to wear shades!"

In the Spring semester of her senior year, as they were driving back from a weekend visit to friends who had just moved to a popular resort town, DeShawn, who was driving, lost control of the car which flew off the road, down a short embankment, and struck a large oak tree. DeShawn was killed instantly and Shanneesha sustained serious injuries. As she told her counselor some weeks later, "When I came to I was kind of hazy, but I looked over and knew he was dead—I couldn't even recognize him."

Shanneesha came to counseling with many difficulties, including significant symptoms of PTSD, depression, but a core issue for her was a simple question. "Why did God let this happen to DeShawn and me? I even wonder if maybe he actually caused it to happen." Prior to the accident, they both had shared what she described as a

> simple Bible-based faith. I believed that God would make the righteous people, those who tried to live by his word, prosper and have his protection. We had tried to live right, and we believed, and we had faith, and look at me now. Before, things made sense and the purpose of my life was clear—to live by faith, to live a Christian life, and to follow Jesus. What kind of sense can that make for me now? Nothing makes sense to me anymore. My life is pretty much a big, black, empty hole.

During one early session, she looked directly at her therapist and asked, "So how is it possible for me to continue to believe in a good and loving God when he treats his faithful children like he treated me and DeShawn?"

Existential Issues in the Aftermath of Trauma

The existential tradition argues that important core beliefs about the meaning and purpose of life, and on the reality that we all are mortal, are important to all human beings. Included in the fundamental existential concerns are the following. We are mortal and must face death—how should that affect how we live? Finding meaning and purpose in life is the responsibility of each person, and discovering meaning and purpose in life are of central importance to each person (Frankl, 1963; Yalom, 1980, 2009). Our experience has been that clients dealing with trauma often raise questions in these domains.

Many of the kinds of circumstances that lead clients to seek help can involve direct reminders of human mortality. Clearly this was the case with Shanneesha's tragic situation. From the existentialist point of view, the human being's status as mortal may be a driving force for psychological problems directly (Yalom, 1980, 2009). Even if this is not the case, clients whose difficulties have reminded them of their own mortality, or the mortality of loved ones, may bring existential questions into therapy.

The specific content of people's answers to the central existential questions will differ, but most human beings have developed some answers to those questions, and if they have not, they may well try to find answers to them in the wake of tragedy and loss. Unlike empirical beliefs, such as those about the predictability and controllability of one's life, existential assumptions are not directly amenable to empirical disconfirmation. The accident that takes one's fiancé shows that the world is not predictable, but it cannot directly demonstrate that life has no meaning. This protection from empirical disconfirmation may make spiritual and religious assumptions particularly capable of accommodating tragedy and loss into the pre-existing assumptive world. Nevertheless, as Shanneesha's experience indicates, even important existential assumptions are not impervious to question when tragedy strikes.

Another major assumption of the existential perspective is that each person is alone in the universe and each one has the responsibility for "creating one's own self, [and] destiny" (Yalom, 1980, p. 218). Many people facing life crises experience the sense of being disconnected from other people. As the research on social support indicates, positive connections to other people can be psychologically helpful to persons dealing with traumatic events (Yuval & Adams, 2011). However, the existential point of view can serve to remind clinicians that concerns about one's ultimate aloneness may add to the psychological burdens of people facing crises. Conversely, recognition and acceptance of one's aloneness can also offer opportunities for major positive changes in one's philosophy of life.

Another emphasis of the existential tradition is the centrality of the quest for purpose and meaning in life. "What is the purpose of my life?" is viewed in this framework as perhaps the single most important question human beings can ask, and it can be an essential question for people who have experienced traumatic events (Frankl, 1963). Clients will not necessarily ask the question this broadly or in this particular way, but some aspects of this question may arise in treatment. Why did this happen? Why did this happen to me? What sense does this make? Viewing these questions from the framework of our model of posttraumatic growth, these questions reflect the psychological discomfort experienced by the person who has had core beliefs challenged, and who has not yet found a way of satisfactorily coming to terms with what has happened. Helping clients address the questions they may have about the causes, reasons, and the broader meaning of what has happened can provide the opportunity to help clients develop a more satisfactory assumptive world, and one that in the future can be more resilient to subsequent major stressors (Janoff-Bulman, 2006).

Shanneesha was still struggling with broad existential questions. Her core beliefs were religious, and they had provided answers to those existential questions in ways that had been previously satisfactory. But they no longer were providing such answers, and part of the focus in treatment was to go with her on the journey of rebuilding her understanding of what her beliefs should be about the purpose of her life and how to live it.

In work with clients like Shanneesha who are addressing existential questions, helping the client to learn to engage in what has been called dialectical thinking may provide therapists and clients with additional ways of thinking about what has happened. "Dialectical thought ... is the ability to recognize and work effectively with contradictions" (Daloz, Keen, Keen, & Parks, 1996, p. 120). There are a variety of ways in which the confrontation with suffering leads people to increase their ability to use and develop comfort with apparent contradictions (Erbes, 2004). For example, people may need to learn that they have new limitations imposed by the traumatic event, but that they also have new possibilities; a person may be able to do less in some ways but more in others, and people may have experienced losses but also gains. A widely quoted summary of living with these kinds of contradictions is the "serenity prayer" written by the Protestant theologian, Reinhold Niebuhr: "God grant me the strength to change the things

I can, the serenity to accept those I cannot change, and the wisdom to know the difference." For some persons in the wake of trauma, the new way of thinking may lead them to see, perhaps paradoxically, that they must accept what has been lost, but also to reconize the possibility that something may have been gained. Of course, this is the essential experience of PTG.

Traumatic events raise existential issues and they may also offer the possibility of developing a revised set of core beliefs that may be more resilient in the face of future life challenges. The worldviews of many psychotherapy clients will include spiritual or religious components. Although we will next turn our attention to this dimension of life, the discussion may also prove useful as a general framework for helping clients who are committed atheists or agnostics; for those clients a semantic focus that deals with existential matters that are not discussed with religious and spiritual terminology will be the appropriate alternative.

Spirituality and Religion in the Aftermath of Trauma

What Should Clinicians Know about Religion or Spirituality in General?

The short answer is—a lot. This is particularly the case where clients are likely to bring their religion into treatment, for example the United States and regions of South America and Africa. The typical program in clinical training does not devote much attention, if any, to spiritual or religious matters raised by clients and many clinicians are understandably hesitant about their competence to deal with religious issues articulated by their clients (Crook-Lyon, O'Grady, Smith, Jense, Golightly, & Potkar, 2011, Dec 5). Clinicians whose clients regard spiritual matters as important to their traumatic situation need to know much in this domain. To be appropriately comfortable with these issues in therapy, clinicians should study the religions and spiritual systems of their clients, even if they are not themselves religious or spiritual.

No individual can know everything and no psychotherapist can develop the necessary familiarity, in advance, with the cultural traditions and spiritual traditions of all of their clients. This is another example where expert companions can be open about their ignorance and lack of experience with particular traditions, and ask the client for tutoring in the beliefs, experiences, and practices that are important. Consider now how Shanneesha's struggles are addressed by a clinician who strives to be an expert companion.

S: This whole situation has made me wonder about all the stuff I grew up with. I always wanted to honor my parents' beliefs, and they became my beliefs, too. But now I think of them more like their beliefs and not mine. I am not sure what to believe anymore.

T: You were comfortable with these beliefs, until recently?

S: Absolutely, although about when I came to college I started to wonder a little about things. But I put any doubts out of my mind.

T: After that the accident happened you started to wonder even more.

S: Right. Some things just don't seem to fit for me anymore, and when I started telling my parents this, they got real defensive and stuff, and I just stopped bringing it up after a while.

T: So that's when it started to seem like their beliefs and yours might not be just the same.

S: Yeah, well after the accident then things really started to hit me, and my parents didn't understand why I would question God about what happened to DeShawn, and it all got really confusing and I'm still confused.

T: Help me understand better what you were taught.

S: Well, I was home schooled and we would have Bible time every day, so I got to know the Word really well. I know a lot about it, and can tell you where everything is in the Bible. And me and my parents, we believe the Word *as written*, you know, not some interpretation of it. We don't believe in interpretation. And my parents, it drives them crazy when people say something about a literal interpretation of the Bible. They say, there should be no interpretation at all. Just read it! So anyway, we believe in Jesus Christ as our Savior and he will come in the Rapture to get us, and a lot of people aren't going to make it.

But I came to college, which by the way my parents were really against, but I couldn't get a marketing degree at a Bible College; so that's how I ended up here. Anyway, I came to college and I really liked some people I met, but they didn't believe the same things I always have, and one was even a Jew! So, I really started liking people and thinking how could God leave them behind in the Rapture, that would be so sad. You see, I've always been around people like us, good Christians, and I never really thought about liking people much who weren't. I figured they would be immoral, but they weren't. And then when Sherry was killed in that accident, and she was just the sweetest girl, I started thinking, how could she not be saved? Would God not want someone like that? And I started thinking that even if she was a Catholic, maybe she is saved anyway. But that's real different from how I was raised. But then, when DeShawn was killed, it's really gotten bad, because as I told you before, we always believed we would be protected in our faith, and that God would favor us in our life together for being believers. Now, I think DeShawn is with God—I know that, but why would God separate us like this? We would be a couple in this world who would do His will. We were going to be, together the two of us, a force for God! We had the Spirit in our relationship! Now what? I am trying to discern His will, but how could it be this? It's not only so sad and lonely without DeShawn, it's that I don't know how to live. How do I live without DeShawn?

T: And how do you live without knowing God's will?

Here we can see that Shanneesha is dealing with various losses. She has lost her fiancé, DeShawn. By losing him she has also lost the plan for her life that she and DeShawn had made together. She has also suffered a blow to her core beliefs about God's role in protecting believers and providing a good life. There were some indications of questioning of these beliefs with the death of her friend Sherry, but Sherry was not a real believer in her eyes. So she wondered how Sherry, a kind person, would not be favored. This she might have seen as tragic, a consequence of Sherry's lack of belief in the kind of religion that Shanneesha had been taught. But DeShawn was truly a believer and his death was a major challenge. For the clinician to help explore her dilemma, there must be a good understanding of Shanneesha's beliefs. Being willing to listen and learn about these beliefs will allow the clinician to be a better expert companion.

T: Of course I wasn't raised in your family and your religious tradition. So we might need to talk about it more.

C: I can tell you lots of things about the Word.

T: You've already helped me in your description of your beliefs so far. So, when you are taught that only people who believe like your parents will be saved, and then you meet other people who seem moral and kind, and think they won't be saved, it is hard to reconcile that.

C: Right.

T: Especially after Sherry died.

C: Right. Maybe not until Sherry died did I really think of this.

T: What would your parents say about Sherry?

C: She's in Hell.

T: That's something you are having trouble with.

C: That just upsets me so much. I think of that and I start to cry. If she has to be dead, I want her to be with Jesus.

T: Is there any way for that to be?

C: Not from what my parents say.

T: I suppose you pray for her.

C: Yes, I do. I hope that helps her.

T: You believe in prayer?

C: Oh, yes.

T: What do your parents say about that.

C: I can't pray her into heaven. That's God's business.

T: These are hard things to sort out, aren't they? Then DeShawn's death makes it much harder to sort things out about God's will. You and DeShawn, unlike Sherry, believed. Is that how it went for you?

C: I can't understand why this is getting so hard for me. I wish I could just go back to believing again. It's like I am becoming an unbeliever. It's bad enough about Sherry, and now I am getting worried about myself.

T: I can tell you are very earnest about wanting to know God and understand how to live your life accordingly. I think that must count for a lot. It would be different if you didn't care, but you obviously do. Knowing God seems to be the central concern of your life, and perhaps He is pleased that you are so much wanting to know Him. I am not a preacher, but that is what I am thinking.

This brief example suggests at least two things. First, the clinician was honest about his ignorance and, in the role of a companion, asked the client for help in understanding things. Second, while acknowledging a lack of expertise in this particular religious tradition, the clinician was still able to provide support for the client, and to continue to do so, in spite of that lack of expert knowledge.

An additional and readily available resource for finding out about a religion with which clinicians are not familiar, is to seek some tutoring from a local leader of the particular religious organization or group to which clients belong. We have found clergy and religious leaders from all denominations to be very willing to help us understand their religious communities better. In doing so, however, it is important to keep in mind the very wide diversity of experiences and views that are present even within groups that use the same names. For example, in the United States, there are at least 11 denominations that call themselves Presbyterian. Within that limited religious category there are widely differing views on a variety of religious and ethical matters, including whether women can be ordained, and whether gay persons are allowed to serve in leadership capacities. It is important, as we emphasized in Chapter 3, to understand clients in uniqueness of their experiences and individual sociocultural worlds and not to see them only as members of a broad category of people.

What Should the Clinician Know About the Client's Spirituality?

Although there are no unambiguous ways of determining whether a counselor has sufficient competence to be able to help clients whose spiritual and religious culture may be quite different from their own, our bias is to caution clinicians not to sell themselves short. If the clinician has successfully established a sound therapeutic relationship with a client, *clinicians should not abandon the client because of the fear they lack sufficient expertise about the client's spiritual culture.* Expert companions who have established a sound relationship can be of great help to clients dealing with major life crises, even if they have to rely on their clients to help them learn about and understand the difficult experience within a social, religious, and cultural context that may be quite different from their own. The expert companion is ready to learn, and that willingness may itself help build a relationship of trust and mutual respect with the client.

In some circumstances, the clinician may want to conduct a systematic evaluation of the client's religion or spirituality. Inventories are essential in the scholarly investigation of spirituality and religion in the context of coping with major difficulties. However, our experience is that with most clients, most of the time, quantitative inventories are not necessary for clinical work. Whichever form of assessment the clinician chooses—clinical or psychometric—he or she should always listen for the presence of religious and spiritual themes in what clients reveal.

Dealing with matters in this domain requires great tact, but when clinicians have a good indication that these matters may be important to the client, some form of direct inquiry may be desirable. "To what extent do you see yourself as a spiritual or religious person?" and "To what extent has what you have been going through led you to think about spiritual or religious matters?" are examples of probes that can prove useful. We are not advocating that clinicians conduct this kind of focused assessment of spiritual matters in the first session; we are suggesting that it is important to be alert for signals that such matters are relevant and for opportunities to find out more about the client's spiritual or religious perspective. If clinicians want to be open to the possibility that their clients may experience posttraumatic growth, knowledge of the clients' views and experiences in this area are very important.

The religious and spiritual elements of Shanneesha's worldview had been seriously threatened and in some ways she regarded them as having been invalidated. She was explicitly articulating her struggles in this area. Many clients will not be quite so clear about their experience of cognitive dissonance in the spiritual domain. It is wise for clinicians to listen for indications that their clients' spiritual beliefs have been shaken, shattered, or already modified in the wake of trauma. Many spiritual assumptions are robust to invalidation by life circumstances, but many people exposed to traumatic events experience some degree of challenge to important philosophical assumptions. Having a good sense of what the client's spiritual beliefs were before, and which important assumptions are still being ruminated about, can be helpful in attending to the spiritual matters that emerge in counseling.

Spirituality Can Help in the Wake of Trauma

Spirituality or religion may be irrelevant to many clients, but a significant proportion of people who live in areas of the world where religion is an important component of daily life are likely to bring religious concerns when they seek psychological treatment. There is a variety of ways that religion and spirituality can be helpful to people struggling with very difficult life circumstances.

For people who are part of organized religious groups, the religious community can be a helpful resource in times of crisis (Green & Elliott, 2010; Pargament, 1997). The religious community can provide support in a variety of forms, including emotional support, social activities, social rituals relevant to specific stressful situations (e.g. funerals), and perhaps by the direct provision of services or of material goods. Some North American congregations, for example, have parish nurses on staff whose responsibilities include keeping regular contact with aged members, helping with arrangements for health care visits, and providing direct care when illness creates significant problems.

The assumptions that people may have that their lives are safe, predictable, and controllable are swiftly negated by events such as the loss of a house in a hurricane, a diagnosis of cancer, or a motor vehicle accident. Religious beliefs, however, can be impervious to assaults by life events. They are robust and it can be very difficult, or impossible, for life events to disconfirm them. A person's belief in God, although perhaps shaken by what happens, is not directly contradicted by any set of life circumstances. Shanneesha, for example, was struggling with her understanding of the nature of God, but her belief in God's existence was unchanged.

Core assumptions in the spiritual domain can provide a way to cognitively assimilate major life disruptions. To the extent that the preexisting worldview allows the person to restore cognitive balance, reestablishing the foundations of the assumptive world that has been shaken by a seismic life event, then spiritual beliefs can be helpful in the coping process. There is plentiful evidence that certain kinds of religious and spiritual coping can be helpful in dealing with major life disruptions (Hebert & Schulz, 2009).

Spirituality Can Hurt

A Brazilian proverb says that "every religion is good." However, the available data suggest that this is not necessarily the case. Spirituality can have a negative impact, particularly when the focus is on the way the religious person interprets the negative events that have happened.

Shanneesha, for example, had reached the conclusion that she and DeShawn on the one hand, and God, on the other, had a contract. If they lived the right way, then God would take care of them and make them prosper. Consider how she expresses this and how the expert companion addresses this loss of her clear understanding in her faith.

S: You see, DeShawn and I talked a lot about our faith. It was so wonderful meeting a guy who I could share this with. My parents were so happy I met someone who could support me in my faith and it was like he was part of our family right away. They were kind of surprised that I found him at college because they were really afraid I would go astray there. So it was like perfect. We loved each other so much and were so devoted to the Lord. We made an agreement that we would stay virgins and that we would do our relationship according to the Lord's wishes, because we knew that would bring true happiness for us. We both believed that the Lord knows best about how to love, and if we did it His way, we would be blessed. But now it's like He let us down. In a big way, the biggest. My parents say I have to just accept God's will, but this just can't be His will. I just can't think it is.

T: I imagine your parents may have tried to reassure you that in some way God was not trying to ruin your life, that His will was being done for some divine purpose?

S: Yes, they said that we can't always know God's will because we can't see the big picture, things beyond ourselves. That this is not just about me and DeShawn. They tell me it has to do with more than us, it is about our role in the entire course of life. This is really hard for me to grasp. They are so good at accepting. It's harder for me.

T: Because you lost DeShawn. That may make it harder.

S: It does. A lot. I loved him so much. I always will. Now I have to wait to see him. And what do I do in the meantime? I just can't see the path. My parents say God is leading me, but I don't see the path. It seems like nothing is there, and God just broke things off with me, and just left me.

T: You'd like to believe there is a path for you, one devised by God?

S: Yes, I want to believe that, but it is so hard to think that He would promise me DeShawn and then break the promise.

T: Your parents say no promise is broken, I guess.

S: That's right, they say God didn't promise me DeShawn. It might have felt like it to all of us because it seemed so perfect, but God doesn't set an easy path before us. Look at Job, look at Jonah, look at Jesus! Almost everyone in the Bible has a hard path for God.

T: And you do, too.

S: It seems very hard now. It's hard to see God's blessing.

T: Perhaps in this tragedy, there is something that is ahead for you that will reveal something about this path, that may still show you how to understand God. Like I said before, you seem very devoted to understanding.

S: But my parents warn me that I shouldn't expect to understand everything about God and His will. That would be just for me, like eating from the apple. I need to just go with it. Have faith. I don't need to know. But part of me really wants to know. See how confusing it is?

T: I don't know where all your questions and confusion will take you, but it may be that some combination of acceptance, and your earnest wish to understand, may yield some changes that you may find very valuable and important to you.

From Shanneesha's point of view she and DeShawn had kept their bargain, but God had not. She implied that God is not as trustworthy and as dependable as she believed. If this is the way she is thinking about her tragedy, will it be a positive or a negative coping strategy? The clinician starts to suggest that there may be something positive in engaging the profound challenges to her belief system; at the same time, accepting some things about the situation could produce something of value to her later. The clinician here has to be careful not to urge her to reject her worldview as represented by her family's beliefs, or to simply go back to it, given how Sherry's death, and especially DeShawn's, have challenged it. As an expert companion, the clinician asks Shanneesha to tolerate the ambiguity for the time being, and to continue in this process.

Consider what we know about religious coping that may be relevant here and that could guide the clinician. The empirical data suggest that at least two aspects of religious life can be harmful to psychological adjustment. One way it can be harmful is through the negative response of the person's religious group (Pargament, 1997). The psychological well-being of the person who is part of a spiritual community may be made worse when the community engages in actions that create social costs and deficits for the individual. For example, people who report that their religious communities have offered opposition to a chosen course of action for dealing with a problem, or who have actively criticized the individual's coping efforts, also report lower levels of psychological functioning (Pargament, 1997). When the religious group to which the client belongs engages in negative or hostile social responses, the individual is psychologically worse off for being part of that particular group.

Another way that spiritual attempts to cope may prove to be negative for overall adjustment occurs in the person's own understanding of the traumatic circumstance. If the client views the event as something that God should have prevented, but which "he let happen anyway" as a sign of abandonment, or as a "way of punishing me for my sins and lack of spirituality," then psychological adjustment can be adversely affected (Gerber, Boals, & Schuettler, 2011; Pargament, 1997). Spiritual attempts to cope, then, although they are helpful in many instances, can be negative in some. From an empirical viewpoint, there are some religious interpretations that clients make that may be undesirable when the criterion is distress or maladjustment. But how is the clinician to distinguish good from bad spiritual or religious understanding?

Spirituality: Good or Bad for Posttraumatic Growth?

Two colleagues who are practicing psychotherapists read the summary of Shanneesha's tragedy and an interesting disagreement occurred. One reacted very negatively and indicated that Shannesha's religious faith was clearly immature, unsophisticated, theologically unsound, and that many readers would be offended by it. The other colleague indicated that she thought this was an excellent example for the beginning of the chapter because it raised many of the issues that were being addressed in the chapter. The two colleagues, were, among other things, making judgments about whether Shanneesha's religious views were good or bad. How should a clinician decide if the individual's religious interpretation is good or bad, and whether it is likely to contribute to posttraumatic growth?

Some readers may think that the question is inappropriate, arrogant, or both. A good guiding principle for psychotherapy is that the clinician should generally stay neutral in matters related to values, morality, and spirituality, and this goal, although probably impossible to reach, is a good one—usually. Neutrality and empathic understanding of matters regarding the client's assumptive world are desirable goals for the counselor. However, even professional codes of ethics make value judgments about some forms of client behavior. For example, psychologists are expected not to accept or condone beliefs that significantly limit a person's well-being (American Psychological Association, 2002).

It is imperative that the clinician do everything possible to avoid manipulating the client's views and choices, but psychotherapy is never an entirely sterile enterprise in relation to values and beliefs. There is perhaps no other circumstance in treatment that is as value-laden as when a client wrestles with spiritual and religious issues in the aftermath of a major loss or tragedy. Given that some spiritual interpretations may prove detrimental, the question emerges again: How does the clinician decide if the individual's religion is good?

First, a necessary and cautious disclaimer. This question cannot be thoroughly addressed in brief form, as a brief detour from the discussion of posttraumatic spiritual growth. However, it is an important question to address, even if incompletely. We offer four general ethical rules of thumb as vantage points from which to evaluate the client's spiritual interpretations and experiences. The four rules of thumb are: (a) does psychopathology underlie the religious interpretation or experience (b) beneficence and the common good (c) the client's individual development and psychological well-being (d) the middle path between extremes.

Mental health professionals are trained to recognize clinical syndromes and to classify them using current diagnostic categorizations. It is appropriate to address, and perhaps challenge, the client's religious interpretations when these are clearly reflective of forms of psychological disorders characterized by compulsions, episodes of mood disorders, or manifestations of other kinds of psychopathology (Knapp, Lemoncelli, VandeCreek, 2010). When delusions, hallucinations, and other components of serious psychological disorders are present, their religious content should be addressed as manifestations of the disorder, and treated as part of the larger psychiatric problem. This circumstance would clearly be one where not accepting the client's "religious" interpretations would be appropriate. However, the way the clinician works with these problems is crucial. We still recommend expert companionship in addressing these sorts of problems, rather than being insensitive to the importance of the beliefs to clients, even those who demonstrate serious psychiatric disturbance.

The notion of the *common good* is a challenging one, because different groups of people, particularly in highly diverse societies such as the United States, will likely reach quite different descriptions of what the common good is. In spite of those potential challenges, the general ethical question—to what extent does this interpretation or this course of action contribute to or detract from the common good—may be a useful guide. If the client's religious interpretations and spiritual understandings lead to conceptualizations and actions that tend to contribute to the common good, then the counselor can regard them as desirable. Daloz, Keen, Keen, & Parks (1996, p. 16) suggested that "the common good would include such core elements as global scope, a recognition of diversity, and a vision of society as composed of individuals whose own well-being is inextricably bound up with the good for the whole."

A third rule of thumb for judging the client's religious interpretations and practices includes the view of beneficence, especially toward oneself; do the religious understandings promote the client's own welfare (Knapp, Lemoncelli, &

Vandecreek, 2010)? Do the person's ways of understanding the difficult situation contribute to development and to psychological well-being? For example, does a person's interpretation that her breast cancer is punishment from God, because of "my sexual immorality" contribute positively to her well-being? When a father views the death of his newborn son as punishment for his lack of faith, should the psychologist accept and support his understanding? As previously noted, the available data indicate that negative kinds of religious coping that attribute life's misfortunes to one's sinfulness or to God's punishment, are likely to increase psychological distress. As with the principle of the common good, determining whether or not a particular interpretation is contributing, or not, to the client's well-being and general welfare may be difficult to establish empirically. Nevertheless, it can be necessary for clinicians to consider the impact of spiritual interpretations on well-being, when their clients are trying to come to a spiritual understanding of what has happened.

The fourth rule of thumb comes from the ancient Greek philosopher Aristotle— it is the principle of *the golden mean*. The idea is simple, but its application will be challenging. The central assumption on which this principle rests is that the virtuous path, the morally correct choice, is the one that lies between two extremes; Aristotle referred to those extremes as vices (Aristotle, 2011). The middle course is assumed to be better than the extremes of excess or deficit. The rule of thumb is that, in the context of spirituality and religion, the golden mean lies between the extremes of fanatical devotion on the one hand, and categorical and hostile rejection on the other. As with the previous three rules of thumb, however, the specific application of the principle still requires the sound and wise judgment of the psychotherapist in the specific clinical circumstance.

Posttraumatic Growth and Spirituality in Treatment

It is important to employ the most demonstrably effective treatments for clearly specified psychological difficulties. One of the most effective elements in good psychotherapy with persons dealing with major stressors may be how well the psychotherapist listens to the client (Norcross & Rampold, 2011). Because the domain of spirituality is one in which individuals can experience significant posttraumatic growth, it is important to attend and listen carefully for spiritual and religious themes. The clinician should listen for them and attend to them when they occur, identify the theme when it is there, and label it when appropriate. It is important for the clinician to exemplify accurate empathy in the spiritual domain and not to shy away from identifying these themes when they occur. When Shanneesha articulated the views presented earlier in this chapter, it would be obvious she was talking about religious issues, within a particular kind of Christian belief system. However, such themes may not always be obvious, or even clear.

The father of the young son who committed suicide (see Chapter 1) in one session said, "I just keep going over and over in my mind what role I played in this. Maybe I should have reconciled with his mother. Maybe I should have worked fewer hours. Maybe this is somehow a result of how I have lived my life. Maybe I just should have been a better person."

There is clearly no single correct response for a clinician to make to this man. The client's words do not explicitly articulate spiritual matters, but indirectly they do, in the broadest existential way—how to choose to live one's life. The therapist responded in this way: "You are really struggling with a lot of very burdensome and gnawing unanswered questions. One big question seems to be: How should I choose the way I live my life now?" The content of this exchange is not religious, but the clinician was attending to the possible existential elements in what the man had said. The response, in this case, did help the client focus on the general theme of how to alter life priorities and how to make new choices, which is often a major way clients experience posttraumatic growth. Clinicians should pay attention when spiritual or religious themes emerge and they should not ignore them.

Subsequently, the clinician working with this man at one point asked "How does your son's death fit in with how you understand why things happen in life?" The father said that as a child and young man he had been a traditional Catholic, but his beliefs had changed over the years. He was currently an atheist, but he felt that he needed to pursue what he described as a godless form of spirituality in which he would seek "peace and enlightenment" by simply "doing what is right in life."

There are many spiritual and religious themes that the therapist can attend to and perhaps probe for. These will vary greatly according to sociocultural context, but some that we have encountered include: issues related to mortality, life's purpose and meaning, one's life priorities, fundamental choices about how to live, issues related to traditional religious beliefs and experience, and broad spiritual themes. As with any action on the part of the psychotherapist, probing for these themes should only be done when both the content and the timing are appropriate, and always with the goal of helping the client.

Countertransference Matters and Posttraumatic Growth

Working with traumatized clients can raise challenging questions about existential issues and spiritual matters for the psychotherapist. When working in the domain of religious beliefs and practices, it is important for clinicians to have either worked through their issues in this area, or at least to genuinely be aware that these matters are still unresolved. When clients experience existential distress and anxiety triggered by a traumatic event, perhaps in some way similar to what Shanneesha experienced, these can make salient for therapists their own failure to satisfactorily come to terms with their own existential dilemmas.

In psychoanalytic theory, countertransference refers to the process whereby psychotherapists may play out unconscious conflicts in their relationships with clients. In the value-laden domain of spirituality and religion, clinicians must maintain continual vigilance so that their responses are not fueled by their own needs or anxieties. Clinicians working with clients to enhance the possibility of posttraumatic growth must be aware of their biases about religious and spiritual matters and be aware of their own answers to the fundamental existential questions. They need to be aware of what their own personal, subjective, and experiential reactions are when clients grapple with religious and spiritual matters.

Recall the differing reactions of the two colleagues who commented on our inclusion of Shanneesha's experience. One colleague viewed her theological understandings as immature and unsophisticated, whereas the other thought the description was a helpful case for discussion. The first colleague's response seems to reveal some degree of antipathy for uncomplicated, religiously conservative, views; how might that particular stance affect that clinician's response to Shanneesha and the questions she was raising? Would there be disapproval, a desire to help her move toward a more "sophisticated" version of her beliefs, a temptation to "educate" her, or perhaps a need to expound on why Shanneesha's interpretation would lead to poor coping and lowered psychological adjustment?

As Carl Rogers suggested many years ago, good therapists must be fully and genuinely aware of their true experience moment to moment in psychotherapy (Rogers, 1961). This suggestion seems particularly appropriate when clients espouse religious views and describe religious experiences that are undesirable from the therapist's perspective. The overt response to clients must always be guided by the goal of doing what is best for them. When helping clients explore posttraumatic growth in spiritual matters in the aftermath of trauma, following Rogers' suggestion is of crucial importance.

What is a Good Spiritual Outcome in Posttraumatic Growth?

The ultimate arbiter of whether posttraumatic growth has occurred, the degree to which it matters, and how desirable it is, is the client. If the person's struggle with trauma leads him or her to experience a better understanding of spiritual matters, if the person experiences strengthening of freely chosen spiritual commitments, if the person undergoes an increased sense of deep purpose and meaning in life, or if the person chooses a new and different spiritual path, then there has been a good outcome in growth. We are, of course, making the assumption that the choices and changes are good. Even if the outcomes are not good from the clinician's personal point of view (unless they clearly violate ethics or one of the rules of thumb), if the individual experiences them as good then posttraumatic growth has occurred.

Other sections of this book have discussed ways that growth and distress are likely to coexist, at least for a time. In no other domain of growth is this more true than in the overlapping areas of existential, spiritual, and religious understandings. The data do suggest that there may well be an inevitable dialectic between distress and growth, and between illusion and truth. People who are at the highest levels of resilience, who are very successful at coping with major stressors, and who are able quickly to muster significant resources and defenses to reduce distress may be less likely to experience spiritual or existential posttraumatic growth. People whose philosophies of life are only slightly shaken by traumatic events may be less likely to experience growth than those whose existential and spiritual belief systems cannot readily assimilate, and quickly defend against, the gnawing existential questions that are made salient by the confrontation with suffering, loss, and death. To help a client grow in the aftermath of tragedy, the clinician must help the client confront the ultimate and difficult questions about life. Paradoxically, the expert companion must also be respectful of the positive illusions that protect the client from extreme distress.

What Kind of Clinician are You?

We began the chapter by suggesting that psychotherapists tend to live in a different religious and spiritual culture than most of their clients. In countries such as the United States, where a large proportion of the citizens have traditional views about religion and God, psychotherapists are much more likely than their clients to be theologically liberal or agnostic. Because of this possible cultural divide, it may be useful to think about the kind of clinician that you are, in matters of your clients' religious views. There are four general frames of reference that the clinician can have regarding religious matters. One of those is what might be called *uncritical, naïve acceptance of everything*.

We have taught graduate students in clinical courses for many years and, although by no means a systematic count, our observation is that students in more recent cohorts are more anxious and uncomfortable when clients mention religious matters. Reflecting the systematic surveys of psychologists, our graduate students have, with a few exceptions, described themselves as liberal and nonreligious. Students also show great reluctance to probe when religious matters come up, when probing is judged to be the clinically best alternative for the client. That reluctance can translate into a clinical stance where the clinician naïvely accepts, uncritically, anything the client says that has a religious meaning. As we have seen, there are some religious interpretations that can be detrimental to the well-being of the client and sometimes to others as well. Our general assumption is that clinicians should, indeed, accept and work within the client's worldview, including its religious components. However, a naïve and uncritical acceptance of anything the client says or does in the name of religion may not be the most helpful clinical stance to take.

A second and opposite frame of reference on religion is *antireligious*. Psychotherapists with this orientation are firm in their conviction that there is no higher power of any kind, they are atheists, and they view religion as pernicious and undesirable. Religious matters are assumed to have no place in treatment, and treatment should not involve, in any way, religious resources. Sigmund Freud would clearly fall into this category because, for him, religion was a set of neurotic defenses that the patient should be encouraged to overcome.

A third frame of reference that clinicians may have on the client's religion is that of the *true believer* or *religious exclusionist* (Pargament, 1997). This perspective assumes there is one single truth in spiritual matters, that the therapist has that truth, and that religious truth should guide the counselor's responses in therapeutic practice. This point of view represents only a small fraction of contemporary professionals in the United States and it tends to be viewed by many other clinicians as undesirable and unethical.

The fourth frame of reference, and the one that we find most appealing, probably represents the majority position among clinicians – *pragmatic religious constructivism*. Constructivism rests on philosophical foundations that imply, or directly assume, that no single reality exists. We use the modifier *pragmatic* to suggest that, even if the clinician does make certain assumptions about ultimate truth, the best way to approach the client is to work within the parameters of the clients' assumptive world—because that has practical benefit to the client. From this point of view, when spiritual or religious matters are integral elements of the client's understanding of personal tragedy and trauma, it is desirable for the clinician to enter, respectfully, into the client's religious worldview and to utilize that spiritual understanding to help clients improve and perhaps grow. Unless there are clear indications that the person's way of comprehending and finding meaning in what has happened is clearly undesirable or unethical, this perspective suggests that clinicians should work within the confines of the client's understanding and experience. This perspective is the one adopted by the expert companion.

In some ways, the antireligious and religious exclusionist therapists are similar because both make certain absolute assumptions that will affect how they proceed with clients dealing with major life stressors. To the extent that clinicians taking either of these points of view are paired with clients who share their philosophical and religious beliefs, then no problems are likely to occur. However, when such pairings do not occur, then problems would be anticipated. Given the current beliefs held by many in religious countries, it would be expected that the antireligious therapist in particular would find a clash of perspectives occurring frequently with clients, in a therapeutically very undesirable way.

We advocate the pragmatic constructivist perspective. Our view is that the clinician needs to approach the client's religious or spiritual construction of the world (including atheism and agnosticism) with respect, accept that construction as valid for that person, and work from that particular framework in encounters with the client. We are not suggesting that therapists who have strong, perhaps even absolute belief systems, should not be therapists. We are suggesting that clinicians operating within religious frames of reference that are absolute are more likely to encounter trouble, and will be more likely to produce problems for some of their clients. They will have difficulty being good expert companions and they may miss the opportunity to hear themes of growth in the spiritual domain of their clients' lives.

In Shanneesha's case, clinicians who regard religion as undesirable could have difficulty maintaining neutrality about her religious orientation or they might even view her spiritual issues as undesirable elements that required modification. Clinicians with an exclusionist perspective might be tempted to try to set her theology straight, if it disagreed with theirs. And the naïvely accepting clinician might be unable to guide Shanneesha to explore her own understandings of faith in ways that would be helpful to her. The pragmatic constructivist perspective, however, allows the clinician to work within Shanneesha's understanding of life and within her framework of life meaning, reducing the possibility that the clinician will, either by omission or commission, be ineffective or harmful to her. It would also allow for the possibility of spiritual posttraumatic growth.

nine
Vulnerability, Resilience, and Growth for Expert Companions

Working with clients who have experienced tragic losses, great suffering, or who have been exposed to great horrors is challenging. Although some clinicians specialize in working almost exclusively with people who have experienced traumatic events, most have practices where they will encounter such clients less often. But every practicing clinician is going to have at least some clients who tell stories of great tragedy and unimaginable loss.

The mother who witnesses, in her own back yard, the death of her 8-year-old boy when he trips, falls forward, and a pecan shell lodges in his forehead and kills him instantly. The journalist who for years was held in solitary confinement by the military dictatorship, tortured daily, and who now looks like an old man, although he is only 42. The parents who saw their beloved child wither away and die from the cancer that eventually consumed him. The woman who was severely beaten, sexually assaulted, and is alive only because her attacker thought she was dead. The man who was held hostage in his own home for hours by a man who intermittently pointed his small machine gun at his head and said he was going to pull the trigger.

This chapter will address some of the costs and benefits of working with people who have experienced major life crises. The chapter will first examine the possible negative effects of clinical work with people who have experience trauma. Next, the chapter will look at the positive consequences that can come from working with such clients, and the final section will provide recommendations for clinician self-care.

Negative Effects of Trauma Work

A variety of terms and constructs have been used to describe the various ways in which one's work demands in general, or one's work with survivors of traumatic events in particular, can negatively affect psychological well-being. The most common terms in the literature are burnout, vicarious traumatization, secondary traumatic stress, and compassion fatigue.

Burnout is the broadest of these and it describes feelings of "exhaustion, feelings of cynicism and detachment from the job, and a sense of ineffectiveness and lack of accomplishment" (Maslach, Schefeli, & Leiter, 2001, p. 399). Vicarious traumatization describes changes clinicians may experience as a result of working with trauma survivors, with a focus on cognitive factors. This term describes negative changes in the clinician's assumptive world, particularly in the domains of self, views of others, and understanding of the world (McCann & Pearlman, 1990). Compassion fatigue and secondary traumatic stress are expressions that tend to be used interchangeably (Elwood, Mott, Lohr, & Galovski, 2010; Figley, 2002). These terms describe symptoms of PTSD that clinicians develop as a result of their exposure to their clients' stories of traumatic suffering. Although all of the previous terms can be distinguished by their definitions and by their operationalizations, the discussion here will not focus on each concept separately. Rather, the focus will be on the broad question of the kinds of negative psychological impact that working with survivors of major life crises can have.

How prevalent are negative consequences for clinicians who work with survivors of traumatic events? Because there are no studies with samples that accurately represent the whole population of working clinicians, with their varied professional backgrounds, affiliations, caseloads, and client types, any answer to the question must be tempered with caution. But the available data do suggest two reliable answers. First, clinical work with persons who have experienced traumatic events can negatively affect clinicians. Second, only a minority of clinicians are negatively affected by their work. For example, a survey of trauma therapists in the United States found that fewer than 15 percent reported significant compassion fatigue or burnout (Craig & Sprang, 2010). Other studies have reported somewhat higher rates of negative responses in clinicians who have worked with survivors, but the majority of responding clinicians has typically indicated that they do not have vicarious traumatization or compassion fatigue (Figley, 2002).

There are several risk factors for negative responses to trauma work. One risk factor for negative reactions from work with survivors of major life crises is to be a beginning therapist. Therapists who are earlier in their careers and who have spent a shorter time doing such clinical work seem to be at greater risk than experienced clinicians who have spent longer periods of time in clinical work (Devilly, Wright, & Varker, 2009; Ellwood, Mott, Lohr, & Galovski, 2010). Beginning clinicians can face a variety of stressors unrelated to their work with trauma survivors, including adapting to new organizational and occupational challenges and roles, and beginning with lower status in their work roles than more senior and experienced colleagues. These findings suggest that clinician self-care is something that younger and less experienced therapists should be particularly attentive to.

As most clinicians know, a general rule of thumb for assessing the probability that a particular person will develop posttraumatic stress symptoms is the strength of the traumatic dose. The more intense and severe the traumatic experience, and the longer the duration of the exposure to the traumatic circumstances, the higher the probability that symptoms will occur. A similar rule of thumb applies to clinicians. The more graphic, horrible, and intense the stories that clients tell, and the longer clinicians are exposed to those intense and horrible accounts, the greater the risk for clinicians to develop negative psychological reactions from their work (Brady, Guy, Poelstra, & Brokaw, 1999).

Clinicians who are themselves trauma survivors may also be at greater risk for negative psychological reactions produced by their work (Baird & Kracen, 2006). This may be the case especially when the client's experience raises unresolved issues for the therapist. For example, clinicians who are themselves survivors of violent sexual assaults may find themselves becoming seriously affected when the narratives of clients elicit difficult memories and strong emotions that may be connected to their own personal experiences with assault.

Clinicians who are early in their clinical careers, who have repeated exposure to client stories that involve intense and horrible graphic details, and who are themselves survivors of trauma, especially when clients are struggling with traumatic events similar to the one experienced by the therapist, are at increased risk for burnout and compassion fatigue. But it is important to keep this risk in perspective. The majority of clinicians, even those who have one or more of the risk factors, are not likely to experience negative psychological responses to their work. When adverse reactions to clinical work do occur, they tend to be relatively mild (Brady, et al., 1999). In addition, clinical work may also provide the opportunity for positive changes that can be set in motion by the very same client experiences that can place clinicians at risk for negative reactions.

The Positive Side of Clinical Work: Satisfaction and Growth

Although satisfaction with one's profession is not limited to clinical work, there may be some elements of that work, particularly for clinicians whose clients are struggling with the aftermath of major life stressors, that offer unique satisfaction. Compassion satisfaction is one of the ways that clinical work can have positive effects on the therapist. Compassion satisfaction describes the pleasure derived from doing clinical work, whether the pleasure is derived from direct work with clients, or from other aspects of clinical work (Horrell, Holohan, Didion, & Vance, 2011). Available evidence suggests that compassion satisfaction may be more prevalent than negative reactions to clinical work (Sprang, Clark, & Whitt-Woosley, 2007) and that clinicians with more years of clinical experience tend to report higher levels of compassion satisfaction than beginning therapists (Craig & Sprang, 2010).

In addition to significant satisfaction with their work, clinicians who work with persons dealing with very difficult circumstances may also experience vicarious posttraumatic growth (Arnold, Calhoun, Tedeschi, & Cann, 2005; Horrell, Holohan, Didion, & Vance, 2011). Listening to the life stories that clients tell them may change clinicians in a variety of positive ways.

One way clinicians may be changed by their work is through listening to clients' accounts of their heroic struggle and survival. The courage some clients display in the face of great challenges may be an inspiration to clinicians (Pearlman & Saakvitne, 1995). The simple knowledge that the client was exposed to horrible circumstances, was not destroyed by them, or in some way experienced growth from the struggle, may provide a chance for clinicians to regard human beings in general, and perhaps themselves in particular, as having sources of strength on which they themselves may be able to draw. As the writer Allen Rucker has put it, clinicians may indirectly learn that they may have "more emotional grit … and resolve … than you imagine … you are not the weak sister you think you are" (Rucker, 2007, p. 226).

At the same time, however, clients' stories show clinicians, unambiguously, that people are vulnerable to tragedy and loss. The stories clients tell of their tragedies may help clinicians understand more fully the paradoxical dialectic that many clients learn. Empathic understanding can lead clinicians to realize that, as human beings, they are more vulnerable to loss than they had hoped, but perhaps also that human beings are stronger than they had imagined possible. As the struggles clients have with overwhelming difficulties unfold, clinicians may become more able to appreciate the inevitable reality that life offers the possibility of great challenge and loss, but also that there are strengths that are discovered and developed in the struggle with those traumatic events.

Sometimes this truth, that we are all vulnerable, becomes reality for clinicians. The lessons that expert companions have learned from their clients can then be especially useful. A friend and colleague who had done groups for bereaved parents confronted the tragic death of her own child. She soon recognized that working for years with other parents who had experienced that same loss had taught her valuable lessons. She had seen people survive this, so she had hope for herself. She had seen the widely different ways that people coped and she knew that she could choose her own way from all that she had learned from the parents she was trying to help. She was used to confronting pain in others, so she was able to allow herself the freedom and courage to confront her own. The knowledge she had garnered indirectly had taught her also that she had to go through her own pain. But she knew she could survive it.

Work with persons dealing with highly challenging life circumstance can also offer clinicians the opportunity to experience positive change in their own worldviews and philosophies of life. The stories of grief, loss, tragedy, and horror that clients tell can provide a challenge to the assumptive world in ways quite similar to those experienced by persons confronting trauma directly. Vicarious exposure to trauma, as the research on compassion fatigue and vicarious traumatization suggests, can challenge core beliefs and lead to negative changes. But there is also the possibility of vicarious growth as the client's experience leads clinicians to reexamine their own philosophies of life. The confrontation with existential issues may raise these issues for the clinician too.

The client's struggle can raise existential issues for the clinician that are not necessarily pleasant. It is good for the clinician to confront the fundamental questions of existence (Yalom, 1980, 2009) because when they are raised by clients they may raise the clinicians' level of psychological discomfort. Confronting existential issues is inevitable and necessary for people working with clients who have faced traumatic events. To the extent that clinicians are led by the experience of their clients to address these questions openly and honestly, that in itself could be regarded as a form of growth arising from clinical work.

A common element of the experience of posttraumatic growth is a reevaluation of, and sometimes a shift in, life priorities. As clinicians listen to the stories of trauma their clients tell, clinicians may find themselves thinking about their own priorities and making some conscious choices about what is really important to them. For example, working with groups of bereaved parents frequently makes group leaders, who are themselves parents, more aware of how their own child is precious. Working with clients who have experienced tragic losses can lead clinicians to make conscious choices to give higher priority to such things as spending more time with their own families, children, or friends. Each time clients talk about a loss, clinicians may be reminded of what they may still have and what their own priorities should be.

Closely connected to desirable shifts in life priorities is the lesson expert companions can learn, that they should appreciate each day more. "I have learned simply to appreciate each day more" is a common theme in the experience of persons facing a wide range of difficulties. Clinicians can learn the same kind of lesson from listening to what their clients tell them; they can be directed by their clients' difficulties to be more appreciative of many elements of their own lives. There are numerous possibilities. Clinicians who are working with abused spouses may become more grateful for the supportive and kind relationships they are fortunate to experience. Clinicians who are providing support to adult survivors of child abuse may become more appreciative and grateful for the good elements of their own family of origin. The crisis counselor who works with the homeless may appreciate his own modest apartment more. Therapists whose clients may have engaged in abuse may find themselves being more aware of their own need to be good parents, partners, or friends, perhaps working harder at controlling their irritability when they are under stress. As one colleague put it "working with a client who is facing really difficult things usually leads me to do my own priority check, and when I do that I inevitably appreciate my own situation more, at least in some way."

As the research on growth indicates, the struggle with crisis can lead people to experience a stronger connection to other persons. Clinicians' vicarious encounters with the challenges faced by their clients can lead them to also experience a stronger connection to important people in their own lives. "When I get home after doing a group," one leader of support groups for grieving parents said, "I hug my kids just a little bit harder." The vicarious experience can lead clinicians to more fully realize the degree to which maintaining and nurturing connections to their own loved ones is important. There can be a greater appreciation of loved ones, but clinicians may also be induced by their client's accounts to actively strengthen their own ties to other people. "You appreciate them more, but you also want to work on keeping those connections and making them deeper and better." This vicarious exposure can have a double edge, because the traumatic events and the losses experienced by clients also make clear to the clinician that loss and tragedy have the possibility of being part of their lives too. As one clinician has said, "You become aware that each new day offers the possibility of a new beginning, but it also presents the possibility of tragic loss. Because of that, live today to the fullest and don't wait until tomorrow to tell them [loved ones] that you love them."

"No man is an island" is a familiar phrase from the English poet John Dunne. Clinicians, through their own experiences of loss and through their indirect encounters with their clients' losses, may increase their sense of connection to fellow human beings, especially those who suffer (Pearlman & Saakvitne, 1995). Clinicians may not only experience an increased sense of connection with others, but also an increased sense of compassion for others. Clinicians reporting on their own direct exposure to the terrorist attacks of September 11, 2001 indicated that their own experiences had led them to become more connected to, and to feel more compassion for, their own clients' difficulties (Bauwens & Tosone, 2010). Clinicians' sense of general compassion for fellow human beings can increase as a result of work with survivors of traumatic events. Their clients' accounts of loss and suffering can serve as reminders of their own connection to others who experience pain and tragedy, which is the mixed blessing of feeling connected to other human beings who face difficult, sometimes horrible, circumstances. In Donne's phrase, trauma therapists know very well "for whom the bell tolls."

Clinical work with people facing major life crises can raise important existential questions for the therapist, but it can also make salient the connection to others, particularly others who suffer. This combination of heightened existential awareness and enhanced sense of connectedness may lead some therapists to find significant purpose as socially active citizens. One clinician, who specializes in working with adult survivors of child abuse, is involved in political action to increase child abuse prevention programs; he also routinely participates in actions in support of gay, lesbian, bisexual, and transgendered persons. Another clinician, who works occasionally with clients post-trauma, actively works within the organized structure of her religion to improve relations between different ethnic groups. Such purposeful actions, some of them political, may emerge from clinicians' empathic connection to the pain and suffering of their clients. In turn, the participation in actions designed to improve the lives of others may add significantly to the clinician's own sense of purpose and meaning in life.

The Vicarious Slap: Seize the Opportunity

The possibility of posttraumatic growth begins when the foundations of the individual's worldview are severely challenged or shattered. The vicarious experience of the client's trauma provides expert companions with the opportunity to experience a manageable and controlled shaking of the foundations of their own worldviews. Clinicians can experience the shaking of the foundations, with the consequent need to address the possible threats to their core beliefs, without having to pay the high and direct price in suffering that their clients do. The occasional indirect challenges to assumptive worlds that clinicians can feel from their clients' accounts offers the possibility for vicarious posttraumatic growth.

Actor and comedian Richard Belzer, who is a survivor of cancer, has described the diagnosis with the disease as a "cosmic slap in the face." The clinician who works with persons who have been cosmically slapped by their life crises is given the vicarious opportunity to attend to some important life issues without having to suffer directly the pain and sting of the cosmic slap. Clinicians should be prepared to identify, label, reinforce, and encourage posttraumatic growth in themselves, just as they should be prepared to do so in their clients. They should attend to that possibility and take advantage of the opportunity provided by their empathic engagement with clients struggling with traumatic events.

Foundations the Expert Companion Needs

To do their work well, and to enhance the likelihood that their clients will experience posttraumatic growth, there are some important philosophical and spiritual foundations that expert companions need. As Chapter 3 indicated, one of the simplest and most easily achievable foundations is to have a broad and a deep knowledge of the assumptive worlds of their clients. To assist clients in pursuing the possibility of posttraumatic growth, this knowledge is crucial.

The easiest avenue to general knowledge about clients' worldviews is to read about and actively study those views. Clinicians should read about the religious, spiritual, and philosophical traditions from which their clients come. A simple example involves obtaining knowledge of the religious traditions from which their clients typically come, including the views of clients who are atheists, agnostics, or who do not follow the teachings of any particular major religious group. Such broad knowledge does not tell clinicians anything about a particular person, couple, or family. But such knowledge can provide a broad, although tentative, framework for understanding people whose experiences occur within the complex matrix of cultural influences that affect individuals. Such knowledge can provide a helpful framework within which expert companions can seek to learn from clients. What are the paradigms and perspectives about life, and how to live it, that are likely to be held by the people you are going to treat?

Although we have both worked with a wide diversity of clients, in the place that we have done most of our own clinical work a modal client might be described as a moderate to conservative Protestant Republican. There are two obvious general perspectives summarized by that compound description: (a) the Protestant branch of Christianity in its moderate or conservative manifestations and (b) the political tradition of the Republican Party in the United States. When clients fit within those rather broad and heterogeneous categories, clinicians will be more effective if they have a good understanding of the values and assumptions that people who come from those traditions have. Knowing those broad assumptions does not tell anything about a particular client, but that broad knowledge gives clinicians a good starting point.

As we have seen, the general population of the United States tends to be somewhat more religious than are most mental health professionals (see Chapter 8). Knowledge of the main religious traditions of the United States, and of the specific traditions that may predominate among one's clients, are particularly useful for American clinicians to have. Knowledge of such religious beliefs, whether or not they reflect the teaching of a particular organized group, may be particularly important for clients dealing with crises. As demographic and cultural landscapes change, clinicians will encounter a wider degree of heterogeneity in the spiritual and philosophical perspectives of their clients. To be at their best, clinicians will increasingly need to have familiarity with a wide range of traditions, beliefs, and practices.

Clinicians know this already, but a reminder may still be useful. The crucial knowledge that is needed is of the worldview of the *individual persons* for whom they are serving as an expert companion. Becoming familiar with broad differences in culture, for example, "Latino" as compared to "Anglo" is useful. However, knowledge of such broad group differences may inadvertently lead clinicians to respond to clients simply as members of a cultural or ethnic category, rather than as unique people. General knowledge of broad cultural systems of belief is desirable and good. Knowledge about the person's worldview, including the central elements of their core beliefs, however, is crucial.

Much of what clients experience as posttraumatic growth occurs within the parameters of their philosophies of life. For some clients dealing with traumatic events, the elements that become salient are likely to be those that address the existential questions about mortality and meaning in life. The more clinicians know about how clients have answered, or are actively attempting to answer those questions, the more effective they will be in enhancing the possibility of posttraumatic growth.

Clinicians working with trauma survivors often have a sense of satisfaction, honor, and privilege in being able to have clients trust them with their horrific experiences (Horrell, Holohan, Didion, & Vance, 2011). When clients share details of their pain, clinicians can choose to view it as an honor to be chosen to hear it. This honor comes from the raw honesty of clients who choose to share secrets and pain. There are few, if any, times in typical social discourse where such honesty occurs. Even clients' intimates may not hear these accounts because clients may feel the need to protect them. By their demeanor and style, expert companions need to make it clear that they are there for the long haul and they are willing to be fully and authentically present to their clients' honest disclosure of their suffering. This trust can serve as another foundation for the expert companion, by relearning, perhaps with each client, what it means to be fully human.

Readers and audiences of captivating stories and powerful dramatic performances may be personally affected by what they read, see, or hear. It is quite possible that readers and spectators may reconsider their views as a result. In a similar way, empathic clinicians are almost inevitably affected by the narratives of trauma and survival told by their clients. However, the accounts given by clients are much more likely to be emotionally affecting because the survivor is present and the story may be a private one.

We have suggested that the accounts of trauma clients give can force clinicians to consider their own fundamental views of the life well lived. In addition, trauma can raise the question of why some people suffer and some do not. Another good foundation that clinicians need is actively to reflect on their own answers to the existential questions—what does it mean to live a flourishing human life? Whether clinicians have reached their own satisfactory answers or not, they need to get used to talking about these questions with clients, because they are very likely to arise. Some clinicians may need a bit of desensitization to have such discussions if they tend to be very private about such matters. Trauma survivors are often not at all shy about asking questions about life's meaning, the reasons why one should continue to live after experiencing devastating loss, what life priorities should be in the radically changed posttraumatic world, how to meaningfully relate to people around them who appear to be mired in what to the trauma survivor is now trivial, and what kind of God there is, if there is one.

It is important for clinicians to feel comfortable when clients want to explore such existential and spiritual questions; they should be open to various resolutions to such explorations, but open also to the possibility that a satisfactory resolution simply cannot be found. Therapists can short-circuit the process of rebuilding the assumptive world and the process of posttraumatic growth, by being evasive on the one hand, or too sure of the existential answers, on the other. We are convinced that supporting the client in such explorations, when it is appropriate to do so, can be a useful part of what it means to experience posttraumatic growth. To do so most helpfully, the expert companion needs accurately to convey the sense that the survivor is capable of finding a good enough answer.

Although having carefully reflected on the fundamental existential questions is a desirable foundation for clinicians working with people who must face terrible crises in life, it is not necessary for them to have figured out all the cosmic details. It may be better for them to cautiously reveal themselves in their spiritual unsettledness, so the client is not tempted to adopt what may seem as final answers to difficult questions that have been worked out by somebody else. For example, if a grieving client asks the therapist whether she believes in an afterlife, the therapist might say, truthfully, that she is not quite sure, or that she does, but is not quite sure exactly what it will be like.

Expert companions, who work with people who face major life difficulties, who try to help them reduce their level of distress, move toward a life of flourishing, and perhaps experience posttraumatic growth, may be ideally open to spiritual elements, if they become salient for individual clients. They can actively help clients engage in these considerations, are willing to consider various perspectives without becoming defensive, and are willing to talk about their own view while making it clear by their actions that there is no pressure for clients to even consider, much less to adopt them. Clinicians who have some degree of clarity about their own spiritual lives, including atheistic and agnostic perspectives, may be more comfortable in this arena. Therapists who work most effectively in helping people grow from the struggle with traumatic events are likely to be those who are themselves open to the possibilities of growth; they are open to and appreciative of the potentially rewarding effects of working with survivors of loss, tragedy, and grief. To the degree that clinicians approach their work as the expert companions we have described, they are more likely to experience vicarious posttraumatic growth. This is because they take the stance that they will learn from their clients, and they have the courage and patience to listen carefully for the wisdom that may be shared. This kind of work can be demanding, and wise clinicians engage in a variety of ways of taking care of themselves.

Clinician Self-Care

All clinicians, but perhaps those who work with trauma survivors more so, must take good care of themselves. Although it is rewarding in many ways, clinical work can also be challenging. Working with clients who have dealt with highly demanding and sometimes horrible events can take its toll on the clinician. Although as we have seen a negative impact of trauma work tends to be the exception, rather than the rule, it is the wise clinician who establishes a firm foundation for the prevention of difficulties, and for the enhancement of positive effects of clinical work. It is a truism, but bears repeating. To be the most effective at clinical work, clinicians need to stay in good psychological and physical shape. What follows is a brief summary of some of the actions that therapists can take to reduce the chance of significant negative responses from work with survivors of traumatic events. Most of these suggestions are common knowledge to most clinicians, but a brief summary may serve as a useful reminder.

Self-Care as a Professional

One important reminder is that burnout, compassion fatigue, or vicarious traumatization can happen to any clinician—no matter how well trained, resilient, or experienced. It is important to recognize that it can happen to you (Meichenbaum, 2003). Awareness of the possibility and regular self-evaluation are important components of the identification, perhaps prevention, but certainly of early identification of emerging problems from clinical work.

In addition to accurate self-awareness about emerging difficulties, another important element in the prevention of negative reactions is the honest acknowledgment that there are limits to the amount of change and growth that clinicians can help foster, or that clients are capable of experiencing. Although there are a variety of evidence based alternatives from which to choose, even the best treatments may have minimal or no effect on the problems some clients face. This is a reality of all work done by healers, whether in the spiritual, psychological, or physical domains.. Some of our clients are not going to make the kind of progress, or show the kind of growth or improvement, that we would wish for them—and that is an adaptive thought that clinicians need to remember.

A concept developed many years ago may be very helpful in this regard (Rotter, Chance, & Phares, 1972). Although it was given a complex and scholarly name, *minimal goal level*, it speaks directly to the clinician's need to be realistic regarding expectations of positive change in their clients. Minimal goal level refers to the minimal level of performance that a person perceives as satisfactory. The concept was developed in the context of laboratory studies where people were asked to play a little game on which they would receive a score. The minimal goal level was the score that the person received for which they would be willing to tell themselves they had done a good job. In the clinical domain, the question might be—what is the minimal level of progress or posttraumatic growth in a client that you, as a clinician, would regard as reflecting effective therapeutic intervention on your part?

More generally, what is the minimal level of improvement in clients that you would regard as indicating that you are a good therapist? Our guess is that the risk of negative therapist reactions increases as the minimal level of positive change the therapist regards as successful is raised. The more unrealistically high the expectations are, the greater the likelihood of therapist disappointment and negative self-evaluation. As negative self-evaluation persists, one would expect an increased vulnerability to therapist stress reactions and professional burnout. One helpful sounding board, for whether or not clinicians are doing good work, is other clinicians. This is one of the many reasons why regular supervision and regular consultation with colleagues is a very good idea.

All clinicians can benefit from regular consultation with colleagues. However, clinicians who may be especially vulnerable to burnout or compassion fatigue should make sure that regular supervision from experienced and trusted colleagues is part of their routine (Horrell, Holohan, Didion, & Vance, 2011).

Regular supervision is definitely suggested for clinicians who are less experienced, who have themselves survived a major life crisis, and whose caseloads include a high proportion of clients who have faced severely traumatic events and who have serious posttraumatic symptoms. But all clinicians who are working with even one client who has been exposed to horrible life stress should seek appropriate consultation with colleagues.

Another element in professional self-care is to carefully consider the mix of clients in the caseload (Meichenbaum, 2003). It varies with individual circumstance, but every clinician has a limit to the size of caseload that can be handled effectively. In general, the bigger the caseload, the more likely clinicians are to experience negative effects from their work. Where caseloads are heavy, clinicians need to be careful about monitoring their level of professional stress and about engaging in preventive self-care. The mix of types of problems in caseloads is also an important consideration. Clinicians who see mostly persons who have undergone extremely traumatic events are probably more vulnerable than those who see only a small and intermittent number of traumatized clients. Individual clinicians need to monitor the mix of client problems in their caseloads and manage the mix as they consider best for them, or at least as best they can given institutional constraints.

The utilization of effective, empirically supported treatments may be another protective factor for clinicians working with survivors of traumatic events (Craig & Sprang, 2010). The therapists' original training, ongoing supervision, and careful use of both formal and informal continuing education are all ways to maintain up-to-date knowledge of the most effective therapeutic approaches. Being able to implement effective interventions increases confidence and comfort in working with trauma survivors. Expert companions clearly need to maintain the best possible knowledge of what the most current data say about the best ways to try to help clients improve, and perhaps grow.

As was noted above, unrealistically high expectations about the degree to which their clinical help will produce improvements can put clinicians at risk for negative psychological reactions from their work. The reverse, however, is perhaps even more important. Within realistic parameters, clinicians need to systematically and purposefully acknowledge the positive changes that their clients have experienced. This can be something scary to do, but most well trained clinicians are going to help many clients move forward in their search for improved functioning and perhaps growth. And they need to, at least occasionally, take inventory to insure that they are aware of the many clients who have been positively affected by their clinical work.

Personal Self-Care

Most clinicians are already familiar with the suggestions that follow. But despite their knowledge, many still do not engage in good self-care. The main theme in what follows is that it is important to do things that prevent the negative effects of stress in the long run. The recommendations also suggest that is it important to live one's life in a way that maintains a healthy balance between one's professional responsibilities and the broader life outside of work.

Regular exercise has been empirically demonstrated to have very positive psychological effects and to be both a means for preventing the negative effects of stress and for coping with stress when it is actively present. Although for healthy adults regular vigorous, aerobic exercise is recommended, that must be adjusted to the individual's health and general physical condition. Clinicians should not begin programs of exercise without appropriate professional advice and medical consultation. For clinician self-care, the more noticeable benefits of exercise may be psychological. Regular exercise can reduce symptoms of a variety of behavior disorders, and it can increase one's general psychological well-being (Walsh, 2011).

Proper nutrition and healthy sleep patterns are also important components of self-care. The simple reminder is to eat right and get enough sleep. Sleep can be a challenge for clinicians if the stories of their clients produce ruminations at night. To prevent this from happening, clinicians must have a place to "put" these stories—perhaps telling them in supervision sessions. One element of daily life that can be a source of challenge for clinicians is lunchtime. Some may skip it, or eat at their desks, and if they do go out may not choose the healthiest options. Clinicians should beware of developing patterns of clinical practice that do not allow for proper breaks for lunch and that do not include appropriately healthy choices for that meal. For clinicians whose diets include caffeine, care should be taken so that the consumption of it does not interfere with healthy and restful sleep.

Although they differ in their specific focus or practices, the major religions of the world call for at least one day during the week that is devoted to rest or to prayer. A day when people are encouraged, or perhaps religiously required, to refrain from engaging in the usual activities of the rest of the week. Clinicians also need to have time away from their work. They need to take time away from work each week, and they also can benefit from longer times of renewal such as long weekends or vacations.

Although technology makes it difficult to do so, clinicians also need to erect some barriers between themselves and their work. One simple daily practice is to use transition activities between the professional world of clinical work and the personal life away from professional demands. One way to do this is to change clothes when first arriving home from work. Trends in fashion may lead to a lessening of the distinction between "work clothes" and clothes more typically worn at home, but this is a simple activity that can have helpful symbolic meaning both to the clinician and to others with whom clinicians may live.

Once in a workshop, a nurse, who was one of our participants, began to smile as the discussion focused on transition activities between work and home. During the next break, she said that she had not realized the direct impact of those transition activities, and she described her own experience with them. She was a single parent with a 11-year-old son and she typically arrived home from work soon after her son had arrived from school. He usually did not start talking with her as she came in the door in her nurse's uniform. After she had changed her clothes to *civilian* wear, he greeted her warmly by saying, "Hi, Mom. Want some tea now?" Prior to her changing clothes she was *the nurse*; after the change, she was *Mom*.

Clinicians also need to make sure that their lives include recreation and relaxation. As one psychologist told interviewers interested in what helped professionals function well, "Rest, relaxation, physical exercise, avocations, vacations" (Coster & Schwebel, 1997). Referring to avocations, one colleague who conducts stress management workshops is fond of telling his participants that "anything worth doing is worth doing *wrong!*" Clinicians should try to find activities that are unrelated to their professions and that are inherently restorative and enjoyable, regardless of their particular proficiency at them. If the enjoyable activities also provide an opportunity for self-expression, even better. We know clinicians who play soccer, play musical instruments, have herb gardens, read mystery books voraciously, do mediocre carpentry (but really enjoy doing it), and greatly enjoy coaching youth softball. There are lots of possibilities—find some for you!

It is also a good idea to regularly practice some form of systematic mindfulness activity, meditation, or systematic relaxation procedure. Currently, there is great interest in the various uses of mindfulness, especially meditation practices that rely on it (Christopher & Maris, 2010). In addition, there are other approaches to systematically relaxing the body and calming the mind that have proven quite useful in reducing stress, and dysphoric emotional states like sadness and depression (Bei-Hung, Casey, Dusek, & Benson, 2010). Regular practice of any of these different techniques for achieving relaxed bodily states will prove a very useful component of personal self-care.

The restorative power of the natural world can also help reduce stress and improve one's general resilience to it (Hansen-Ketchum, Marck, & Reutter, 2009). Even for persons who do not particularly like the outdoors, we suggest they make some attempt to seek whatever aspects of nature are appealing and available. Large cities and some universities, for example, have botanical gardens that are free and open to the public. Most cities have parks and greenways that are easily accessible. Other possibilities range from overnight backpacking trips in remote areas to simply sitting on the bench in a green area in the middle of a large city.

Another element of self-care to consider it to seek out good humor and to share it with colleagues. Humor can be quite useful as a way to manage stress, but we have some words of caution. First, all humor is not created equal. In general, it is good to avoid humor that insults or demeans individuals or groups. Second, although some humor involves silliness, there is a difference between acting stupidly and being humorous. Wearing a big red fake nose and large red shoes may be funny in some contexts, but it is probably not a good way to introduce humor into the clinical workplace. In some ways, humor may have the same ability that poetry can have—it conveys feelings that individuals may not have been able to put into words. Seek out and share humor that is constructive; in particular, search for humor that addresses professional issues representative of current clinical work. It is important to remember that you do not have to be funny yourself to utilize humor as a means of personal or professional self-care. Cultivate your own ability to perceive humor in difficult circumstances. If you want to share humor, do what Arnie Cann, our colleague and a researcher on humor (Cann, Zapata, & Davis, 2011), recommends: "Do what all the best comedians do for their funny stuff—*steal it!*"

A final suggestion is also well known by clinicians, but we include it as a reminder. Work to develop and maintain supportive relationships with others at home and at work. Try to make sure that the support group outside of work is diverse and not composed solely of clinicians. A general belief that seems common in North American culture, and perhaps elsewhere too, is that relationships should develop and continue spontaneously. The corollary to this belief is that consciously attending to and working on relationships can somehow be manipulative and deceitful. However, it is important for clinicians to be reminded to consciously attend to the most important relationships in their lives—and to actively work at maintaining, nurturing, and improving the relationships that sustain you every day.

Balancing

As somebody has said, life is what happens when you are not at work. As we have seen, most clinicians find their work to be a highly valued part of their lives, a profession that is deeply satisfying and that provides an important contribution to living a full and meaningful life. But some clinicians also find it a challenge to balance demands of work, with the challenges and rewards of their broader lives outside of the professional sphere. There is no easy answer to the question of how to balance professional work and the rest of life. But regardless of how clinicians answer that question for themselves, it will be wise for them to insure that they carve out, and defend with fanatical zeal, time to practice good self-care and time for the many things in life that contribute to living well.

References

Alam, R., Barrera, M., D'Agostino, N., Nicholas, D. B., & Schneiderman, G. (2012). Bereavement experiences of mothers and fathers over time after the death of a child due to cancer. *Death Studies, 36*(1), 1–22. doi:10.1080/07481187.2011.553312

Allen, B. (2002, February 3). In Sylvia's shadow [Review of *Ted Hughes*]. *New York Times Book Review*, p. 12.

Alter, A. L., & Oppenheimer, D. M. (2009). Suppressing secrecy through metacognitive ease: Cognitive fluency encourages self-disclosure. *Psychological Science, 20*(11), 1414–20. doi:10.1111/j.1467-9280.2009.02461.x

American Psychological Association (2002). Ethical Principles of Psychologists and Code of Conduct. *American Psychologist, 57,* 1060–73.

American Psychological Association (2003). Guidelines on multicultural education, training, research, practice, and organizational change for psychologists. *American Psychologist, 58,* 377–402.

Anderson, W. P., & Lopez-Baez, S. I. (2008). Measuring growth with the Posttraumatic Growth Inventory. *Measurement and Evaluation in Counseling and Development, 40,* 215–27.

Ardelt, M. (2003). Empirical assessment of a three-dimensional wisdom scale. *Research on Aging, 25,* 275–324.

Aristotle (2011). *Aristotle's Nichomachean Ethics* (R. C. Bartlett, & S. D. Collins, Trans.). Chicago: University of Chicago Press. (Original work n. d.)

Arnold, D., Calhoun, L. G., Tedeschi, R. G., & Cann, A. (2005). Vicarious posttraumatic growth in psychotherapy. *Journal of Humanistic Psychology, 45,* 239–63.

Aspinwall, L. G., & Tedeschi, R. G. (2010). Of babies and bathwater: A reply to Coyne and Tennen's views on positive psychology and health. *Annals Of Behavioral Medicine, 39*(1), 27–34.

Baird, K., & Kracen, A. C. (2006). Vicarious traumatization and secondary traumatic stress: A research synthesis. *Counselling Psychology Quarterly, 19,* 181–8.

Baker, J. M., Kelly, C., Calhoun, L. G., Cann, A., & Tedeschi, R. G. (2008). An examination of Posttraumatic Growth and Posttraumatic Depreciation: Two exploratory studies. *Journal of Loss and Trauma, 13,* 450–65.

Baltes, P. B., & Smith, J. (2008). The fascination with wisdom: Its nature, ontogeny, and function. *Perspectives on Psychological Science, 3,* 56–64.

Barlow, D. (Ed.) (2008). *Clinical handbook of psychological disorders: A step-by-step treatment manual, 4th Ed.* New York: Guilford Press.

Bauwens, J., & Tosone, C. (2010). Professional posttraumatic growth after a shared traumatic experience: Manhattan clinicians' perspectives on post-9/11 practice. *Journal of Loss and Trauma, 15,* 498–517.

Birkett, D. (2011). Review of "The hero in the mirror." *British Journal of Psychotherapy, 27*(1), 124–6. doi:10.1111/j.1752-0118.2010.01225_4.x

Bloom, S. L. (1998). By the crowd they have been broken, by the crowd they shall be healed: The social transformation of trauma. In R. G. Tedeschi, C. L. Park, L. G. Calhoun (Eds.), *Posttraumatic growth: Positive changes in the aftermath of crisis* (pp. 179–213). Mahwah, NJ US: Lawrence Erlbaum Associates Publishers.

Bonanno, G. A. (2004). Loss, trauma, and human resilience: Have we underestimated the human capacity to thrive after extremely aversive events? *American Psychologist, 59,* 20–8.

Bonanno, G. A. (2009). *The other side of sadness: What the new science of bereavement tells us about life after loss.* New York: Basic Books.

Bormann, J. E., Thorp, S. R., Wetherell, J. L., Golshan, S., & Lang, A. J. (2012). Meditation-based mantram intervention for veterans with posttraumatic stress disorder: A randomized trial. *Psychological Trauma: Theory, Research, Practice, And Policy.* Advanced online publication doi:10.1037/a0027522

Brady, J. L., Guy, J. D., Poelstra, P. L., & Brokaw, B. F. (1999). Vicarious traumatization, spirituality, and the treatment of sexual abuse survivors: A national survey of women psychotherapists. *Professional Psychology: Research and Practice, 30,* 386–93.

Brazilian Institute of Geography and Statistics (1999). What color are you? In R. M. Levine and J. J. Crocitti (Eds.) *The Brazil Reader: History, culture, politics* (pp. 386–90). Durham, NC: Duke University Press.

Brunet, J., McDonough, M. H., Hadd, V., Crocker, P. R. E., & Sabiston, C. M. (2010). The Posttraumatic Growth Inventory: An examination of the factor structure and invariance among breast cancer survivors. *Psycho-Oncology, 19,* 830–8.

Cahill, S. P., Rothbaum, B., Resick, P. A., & Follette, V. M. (2009). Cognitive-behavioral therapy for adults. In E. B. Foa, T. M. Keane, M. J. Friedman, J. A. Cohen (Eds.), *Effective treatments for PTSD: Practice guidelines from the International Society for Traumatic Stress Studies (2nd ed.)* (pp. 139–222). New York, NY US: Guilford Press.

Calhoun, L. G., Selby, J. W., & Abernathy, C. (1984). Suicidal death: Social reactions to bereaved survivors. *The Journal of Psychology, 116,* 255–61.

Calhoun, L. G., Abernathy, C., & Selby, J. W. (1986). The rules of bereavement: Are suicidal deaths different? *Journal of Community Psychology, 14,* 213–18.

Calhoun, L. G., & Tedeschi, R. G. (1999). *Facilitating posttraumatic growth: A clinician's guide.* Mahwah, NJ: Lawrence Erlbaum Associates.

Calhoun, L. G., & Tedeschi, R. G. (2006) (Eds). *Handbook of posttraumatic growth— research and practice.* Mahwah, NJ: Lawrence Erlbaum Associates.

Cann, A., Calhoun, L. G., Tedeschi, R. G., Kilmer, R. P., Gil-Rivas, V., Vishnevsky, T., & Danhauer, S. (2010). The Core Beliefs Inventory: A brief measure of disruption in the assumptive world. *Anxiety, Stress, & Coping, 23,* 19–34.

Cann, A., Calhoun, L. G., Tedeschi, R. G., Triplett, K. N., Vishnevsky, T., & Lindstrom, C. M. (2011). Assessing posttraumatic cognitive processes: The Event Related Rumination Inventory. *Anxiety, Stress, & Coping, 24,* 137–56.

Cann, A., Zapata, C. L., & Davis, H. B. (2011). Humor style and relationship satisfaction in dating couples: Perceived versus self-reported humor styles as predictors of satisfaction. *Humor: International Journal of Humor Research, 24,* 1–20.

Caplan, G. (1964). *Principles of preventive psychiatry.* New York: Basic Books.

Christopher, J. C., & Maris, J. A. (2010). Integrating mindfulness as self-care into counseling and psychotherapy training. *Counselling and Psychotherapy Research, 10,* 114–25.

Cobb, A. R., Tedeschi, R. G., Calhoun, R., G., & Cann, A. (1996). Correlates of posttraumatic growth in survivors of intimate partner violence. *Journal of Traumatic Stress, 19,* 895–903.

Cohen, A. B. (2010). Just how many different forms of culture are there? *American Psychologist, 65,* 59–60.

Corning, A. F., & Bucchianeri, M. M. (2010). Perceiving racism in ambiguous situations: Who relies on easy-to-use information? *The Journal of Social Psychology, 150,* 258–77.

Coster, J. S., & Schwebel, M. (1997). Well-functioning in professional psychologists. *Professional Psychology: Research and Practice, 28,* 5–13.

Craig, C. D., & Sprang, G. (2010). Compassion satisfaction, compassion fatigue, and burnout in a national sample of trauma treatment therapists. *Anxiety, Stress, & Coping, 23,* 319–39.

Crook-Lyon, R. E., O'Grady, K. A., Smith, T. B., Golightly, T., & Potkar, K. A. (2011, December 5). Addressing religious and spiritual diversity in graduate training and multicultural education for professional psychologists. *Psychology of Religion and Spirituality.* Advance online publication. doi: 10.1037/a0026403

Cusack, K., & Spates, C. (1999). The cognitive dismantling of Eye Movement Desensitization and Reprocessing (EMDR) treatment of posttraumatic stress disorder (PTSD). *Journal Of Anxiety Disorders, 13*(1–2), 87–99. doi:10.1016/S0887-6185(98)00041-3

Daloz, L. A. P., Keen, C. H., Keen, J. P., & Parks, S. D. (1996). *Common fire: Lives of commitment in a complex world.* Boston: Beacon.

Davidson, P. R., & Parker, K. C. H. (2001). Eye movement desensitization and reprocessing (EMDR): A meta-analysis. *Journal of Consulting and Clinical Psychology, 69,* 305–16.

Dekel, S., Ein-Dor, T., & Solomon, Z. (2012). Posttraumatic growth and posttraumatic distress: A longitudinal study. *Psychological Trauma: Theory, Research, Practice, And Policy, 4*(1), 94–101. doi:10.1037/a0021865

Delaney, H. D., Miller, W. R., & Bisono, A. M. (2007). Religiosity and spirituality among psychologists: A survey of clinician members of the American Psychological Association. *Professional Psychology: Research and Practice 38,* 538–46.

Descilo, T. T., Vedamurtachar, A. A., Gerbarg, P. L., Nagaraja, D. D., Gangadhar, B. N., Damodaran, B. B., & Brown, R. P. (2010). Effects of a yoga breath intervention alone and in combination with an exposure therapy for post-traumatic stress disorder and depression in survivors of the 2004 South-East Asia tsunami. *Acta Psychiatrica Scandinavica, 121*(4), 289–300. doi:10.1111/j.1600-0447.2009.01466.x

Devilly, G. J., Wright, R., & Varker, T. (2009). Vicarious trauma, secondary stress or simply burnout? Effect of trauma therapy on mental health professionals. *Australian and New Zealand Journal of Psychiatry, 43,* 373–85.

Dohrenwend, B. S. (1978). Social stress and community psychology. *American Journal of Community Psychology, 6,* 1–15.

Doka, K. J. (1995). Coping with life-threatening illness: A task model. *Omega: Journal of Death and Dying, 32*(2), 111–22. doi:10.2190/0WEH-QUBG-67VG-YKJK

Elwood, L. S., Mott, J., Lohr, J. M., & Galovski, T. A. (2011). Secondary trauma symptoms in clinicians: A critical review of the conduct, specificity, and implications for trauma-focused treatment. *Clinical Psychology Review, 31,* 25–36.

Erbes, C. (2004). Our constructions of trauma: A dialectical perspective. *Journal of Constructivist Psychology, 17,* 201–20.

Erikson, E. H. (1963). The Golden Rule and the cycle of life. In R. W. White (Ed.), *The study of lives: Essays on personality in honor of Henry A. Murray* (pp. 412–28). New York: Atherton Press.

Fava, G. A. (1996). The concept of recovery in affective disorders. *Psychotherapy and Psychosomatics, 65*(1), 2–13.

Fava, G. A., & Ruini, C. (2003). Development and characteristics of a well-being enhancing psychotherapeutic strategy: Well-being therapy. *Journal of Behavior Therapy and Experimental Psychiatry, 34*(1), 45–63. doi:10.1016/S0005-7916(03)00019-3

Feigelman, W., Jordan, J. R., & Gorman, B. S. (2009). How they died, time since loss, and bereavement outcomes. *Omega: Journal of Death and Dying, 58*(4), 251–73. doi:10.2190/OM.58.4.a

Figley, C. R. (2002). Compassion fatigue: Psychotherapists' chronic lack of self-care. *Journal of Clinical Psychology, 58,* 1433–41.

Fiske, A. P. (2002). Using individualism and collectivism to compare cultures. *Psychological Bulletin, 128,* 78–88.

Foa, E. B., Hembree, E. A., & Rothbaum, B. (2007). *Prolonged exposure therapy for PTSD: Emotional processing of traumatic experiences: Therapist guide.* New York: Oxford University Press.

Foa, E. B., Keane, T. M., Friedman, M. J., & Cohen, J. A. (2009). *Effective treatments for PTSD: Practice guidelines from the International Society for Traumatic Stress Studies (2nd ed.).* New York, NY US: Guilford Press.

Frankl, V. E. (1963). *Man's search for meaning.* New York: Pocket Books.

—(1988/1969). *The will to meaning: Foundations and applications of logotherapy.* New York: Frankl, V. E. World.

Frazier, P., Tennen, H., Gavian, M., Park, C., Tomich, P., & Tashiro, T. (2009). *Psychological Science, 20,* 912–16.

Gallup.com (June 3, 2011). More than 9 in 10 Americans continue to believe in God. www.gallup.com/poll/147887/americans-continue-believe-god.aspx.

Gilbar, O., Plivazky, N., & Gil, S. (2010). Counterfactual thinking, coping strategies, and coping resources as predictors of PTSD diagnosed in physically injured victims of terror attacks. *Journal of Loss and Trauma, 15,* 304–24.

Gomes, P. (1996). *The good book.* New York: William Morrow.

Green, M., & Elliott, M. (2010). Religion, health, and psychological well-being. *Journal of Religion and Health, 49,* 149–63.

Groleau, J. M., Calhoun, L. G., Cann, A., & Tedeschi, R. G. (2012). The role of centrality of events in posttraumatic distress and posttraumatic growth. *Psychological Trauma: Theory Research, Practice and Policy,* Advance online publication doi:10.1037/a0028809.

Gunty, A. L., Frazier, P. A., Tennen, H., Tomich, P., Tashiro, T., & Park, C. (2010). Moderators of the relationship between perceived and actual posttraumatic growth. *Psychological Trauma: Theory, Research, Practice, and Policy, 3,* 61–6.

Habermas, T., & Bluck, S. (2000). Getting a life: The emergence of the life story in adolescence. *Psychological Bulletin, 126,* 748–69.

Hansen-Ketchum, P., Marck, P., & Reutter, L. (2009). Engaging with nature to promote health: New direction for nursing research. *Journal of Advanced Nursing, 65*, 1527–38.

Hasenkamp, W., Wilson-Mendenhall, C. D., Duncan, E., & Barsalou, L. W. (2012). Mind wandering and attention during focused meditation: A fine-grained temporal analysis of fluctuating cognitive states. *Neuroimage, 59*(1), 750–60. doi:10.1016/j.neuroimage.2011.07.008

Hebert, R., & Schulz, R. (2009). Positive and negative religious coping and well-being in women with breast cancer. *Journal of Palliative Medicine, 12*, 537–45.

Hensley, P. L. (2006). Treatment of bereavement-related depression and traumatic grief. *Journal of Affective Disorders, 92*(1), 117–24. doi:10.1016/j.jad.2005.12.041

Herman, J. L. (1992). *Trauma and recovery.* New York: Basic Books.

Hill, P. C., & Pargament, K. I. (2008). Advances in the conceptualization and measurement of religion and spirituality: Implications for physical and mental health research. *Psychology of Religion and Spirituality, S*, 3–17.

Hobfoll, S. E., Hall, B. J., Canetti-Nisim, D., Galea, S., Johnson, R. J., & Palmieri, P. A. (2007). Refining our understanding of traumatic growth in the face of terrorism: Moving from meaning cognitions to doing what is meaningful. *Applied Psychology: An International Review, 56*(3), 345–66. doi:10.1111/j.1464-0597.2007.00292.x

Horrell, S. C. V., Holohan, D. R., Didion, L. M., & Vance, G. T. (2011). Treating traumatized OEF/OIF veterans: How does trauma treatment affect the clinician? *Professional Psychology: Research and Practice, 42*, 79–86.

Jain, S., Shapiro, S. L., Swanick, S., Roesch, S. C., Mills, P. J., Bell, I., & Schwartz, G. R. (2007). A randomized controlled trial of mindfulness meditation versus relaxation training: effects on distress, positive states of mind, rumination, and distraction. *Annals Of Behavioral Medicine, 33*(1), 11–21. doi:10.1207/s15324796abm3301_2

Janoff-Bulman, R. (1992). *Shattered assumptions.* New York: The Free Press.

Janoff-Bulman, R. (2006). Schema-change perspectives on posttraumatic growth. In L. G. Calhoun & R. G. Tedeschi (Eds). *Handbook of posttraumatic growth* (pp. 81–99). Mahwah, NJ: Lawrence Erlbaum Associates.

Jordan, H. (2000). *No such thing as a bad day.* Atlanta, GA: Longstreet.

Joseph, S., Williams, R., & Yule, W. (1993). Changes in outlook following disaster: The preliminary development of a measure to assess positive and negative responses. *Journal of Traumatic Stress, 6*, 271–9.

Jourard, S. M., & Lasakow, P. (1958). Some factors in self-disclosure. *The Journal of Abnormal and Social Psychology, 56*(1), 91–8. doi:10.1037/h0043357

Kahn, J. H., & Hessling, R. M. (2001). Measuring the tendency to conceal versus disclose psychological distress. *Journal of Social and Clinical Psychology, 20*, 41–65. doi:10.1521/jscp.20.1.41.22254

Kaynak, O., Lepore, S. J., & Kliewer, W. L. (2011). Social support and social constraints moderate the relation between community violence exposure and depressive symptoms in an urban adolescent sample. *Journal of Social and Clinical Psychology, 30*, 250–69.

Keane, T. M., Marshall, A. D., & Taft, C. T. (2006). Posttraumatic stress disorder: Etiology, epidemiology, and treatment outcome. *Annual Review of Clinical Psychology, 2*, 161–97.

Kelly, G. (1969). Personal construct theory and the psychotherapeutic interview. In B. Maher (Ed.), *Clinical psychology and personality: The selected papers of George Kelly* (pp. 224–64). New York: Wiley.

Kemeny, M. E., Foltz, C., Cavanagh, J. F., Cullen, M., Giese-Davis, J., Jennings, P., & Ekman, P. (2012). Contemplative/emotion training reduces negative emotional behavior and promotes prosocial responses. *Emotion, 12*(2), 338–50. doi:10.1037/a0026118

Knapp, S., Lemoncelli, & Vandecreek, L. (2010). Ethical responses when patients' religious beliefs appear to harm their well-being. *Professional Psychology: Research and Practice, 41*, 405–12.

Komp, D. M. (1993). *A child shall lead them: Lessons in hope from children of cancer*. Grand Rapids, MI: Zondervan.

Konigsberg, R. (2011). *The truth about grief: The myth of its five stages and the new science of loss*. New York: Simon & Schuster.

Kraus, M. W., Piff, P. K., & Keltner, D. (2011). Social class as culture. *Current Directions in Psychological Science, 20*, 246–50.

La Roche, M. J., Batista, C., & D'Angelo, E. (2011). A content analyses of guided imagery scripts: A strategy for the development of cultural adaptations. *Journal of Clinical Psychology, 67*(1), 45–57. doi:10.1002/jclp.20742

Lindstrom, C. M., Cann, A., Calhoun, L. G., & Tedeschi, R. G. (2011). The relationship of core belief challenge, rumination, disclosure, and sociocultural elements to posttraumatic growth. *Psychological Trauma: Theory, Research, Practice, and Policy. doi: 10.1037/a0022030*

Linley, P. A. (2003). Positive adaptation to trauma: wisdom as both process and outcome. *Journal of Traumatic Stress, 16*, 601–10.

Linley, P. A., & Joseph, S. (2011). Meaning in life and posttraumatic growth. *Journal of Loss and Trauma, 16*, 150–9.

O'Leary, V. E., & Ickovics, J. R. (1995). Resilience and thriving in response to challenge: An opportunity for a paradigm shift in women's health. *Women's Health: Research on Gender, Behavior, and Policy, 1*,121–42.

Maddi, S. (2012). Creating meaning through making decisions. In P. T. P. Wong (Ed.), *The human quest for meaning, 2nd Ed.* (pp. 57–80). New York: Routledge.

Mahrer, A. R. (1996). Existential-humanistic psychotherapy and the religious person. In E. P Shafranske, (Ed.), *Religion and the clinical practice of psychology* (pp. 433–460*).* Washington, DC: American Psychological Association.

Mandel, D. R., & Dhami, M. K. (2005). "What I did" versus "what I might have done:" Effect of factual versus counterfactual thinking on blame, guilt, and shame in prisoners. *Journal of Experimental Social Psychology, 41*(6), 627–35. doi:10.1016/j.jesp.2004.08.009

Martin, L. L., & Tesser, A. (1996). Clarifying our thoughts. In R. S. Wyer (Ed.), *Ruminative thought: Advances in social cognition, Vol. 9* (pp. 189–209). Mahwah, NJ: Lawrence Erlbaum Associates.

Maslach, C., Schaufeli, W. B., & Leiter, M. P. (2001). Job burnout. *Annual Review of Psychology, 52*, 397–422.

McAdams. D. P. (2006). *The redemptive self. Stories Americans live by*. New York: Oxford University Press.

—(2012). Meaning and personality. In P. T. P. Wong (Ed.), *The human quest for meaning, 2nd ed.* (pp. 107–23). New York: Routledge.

McCann, I. L., & Pearlman, L. A. (1990). *Psychological trauma and the adult survivor: Theory, therapy, and transformation*. New York: Brunner/Mazel.

McCaul, K. D., Solomon, S., & Holmes, D. S. (1979). Effects of paced respiration and expectations on physiological and psychological responses to threat. *Journal of Personality and Social Psychology, 37*(4), 564–71. doi:10.1037/0022-3514.37.4.564

McQuellon, R.P., & Cowan, M.A. (2010). *The art of conversation through serious illness: Lessons for caregivers*. New York: Oxford.

Meichenbaum, D. (2003). *A clinical handbook/practical therapist manual for assessing and treating adults with post-traumatic stress disorder*. Waterloo, Ontario, Canada: Institute Press.

—(2006). Resilience and posttraumatic growth: A constructive narrative perspective. In L. G. Calhoun & R. G. Tedeschi (Eds), *Handbook of posttraumatic growth: Research and practice* (pp. 355–64). Mahwah, NJ: Lawrence Erlbaum Associates.

Monson, C. M., Schnurr, P. P., Resick, P. A., Friedman, M. J., Young-Xu, Y., & Stevens, S. P. (2006). Cognitive processing therapy for veterans with military-related posttraumatic stress disorder. *Journal Of Consulting And Clinical Psychology, 74*(5), 898–907. doi:10.1037/0022-006X.74.5.898

Moore, A. M., Gamblin, T. C., Geller, D. A., Youssef, M. N., Hoffman, K. E., Gemmell, L., & Steel, J. L. (2011). A prospective study of posttraumatic growth as assessed by self-report and family caregiver in the context of advanced cancer. *Psycho-Oncology, 20*, 479–87.

Myers, A. L. (January 8, 2012). Hundreds gather in tribute to Arizona shooting victims. *Associated Press.*

Neimeyer, R. A. (2006a). Re-storying loss: Fostering growth in the posttraumatic narrative. In L. G. Calhoun & R, G. Tedeschi (Eds), *Handbook of posttraumatic growth: Research and practice* (pp. 68–80). Mahwah, NJ: Lawrence Erlbaum Associates.

— (2006b). Narrating the dialogical self: Toward an expanded toolbox for the counselling psychologist. *Counselling Psychology Quarterly, 19*, 105–20.

Neimeyer, R. A., Burke, L. A., Mackay, M. M., & van Dyke Stringer, J. G. (2010). Grief therapy and the reconstruction of meaning: From principles to practice. *Journal of Contemporary Psychotherapy, 40*(2), 73–83. doi:10.1007/s10879-009-9135-3

Neimeyer, R. A., Harris, D. L., Winokuer, H. R., & Thornton, G. F. (2011). *Grief and bereavement in contemporary society: Bridging research and practice.* New York: Routledge.

Nisbett, R. E. (2003). *The geography of thought: How Asians and Westerners think differently.* New York: Free Press.

Norcross, J. C., & Wampold, B. E. (2011). Evidence-based therapy relationships: Research conclusion and clinical practice. *Psychotherapy, 48*, 98–102.

O'Leary, V. E., & Ickovics, J. R. (1995). Resilience and thriving in response to challenge: An opportunity for a paradigm shift in women's health. *Women's Health: Research on Gender, Behavior, and Policy, 1*,121–42.

Ovgu, K., Lepore, S., & Kliewer, W. L. (2011). Social support and social constraints moderate the relation between community violence exposure and depressive symptoms in an urban adolescent sample. *Journal of Social and Clinical Psychology, 30*, 250–69.

Pargament, K. I. (1997). *The psychology of religion and coping.* New York: Guilford.

Park, C. L., Cohen, L., & Murch, R. (1996). Assessment and prediction of stress-related growth. *Journal of Personality, 64*, 645–58.

Parkes, C, M. (1971). Psycho-social transitions: A field for Study. *Social Science and Medicine, 5*, 101–15.

Pearlman, L. A., & Saakvitne, K. W. (1995). *Trauma and the therapist: Countertransference and vicarious traumatization in psychotherapy with incest survivors.* New York: W. W. Norton & Co.

Pennebaker, J. W. (1997). *Opening up: The healing power of expressing emotions.* New York: Guilford Press.

Perry, P. L. (1993). Mourning and funeral customs among African-Americans. In D. P. Irish, K. F. Lundquist, & V. J. Nelsen (Eds), *Ethnic variations in dying:* Diversity in universality (pp. 51–65). Washington, DC: Taylor & Francis.

Phoenix, B. J. (2007). Psychoeducation for survivors of trauma. *Perspectives in Psychiatric Care, 43*(3), 123–31. doi:10.1111/j.1744-6163.2007.00121.x

Price, R. (1994). *A whole new life: An illness and a healing.* New York: Plume.

Reik, T. (1948). *Listening with the third ear: The inner experience of a psychoanalyst.* New York: Grove.

Resick, P. A., Monson, C. M., & Rizvi, S. L. (2008). Posttraumatic stress disorder. In D. H. Barlow (Ed.), *Clinical handbook of psychological disorders: A step-by-step treatment manual (4th ed.)* (pp. 65–122). New York, NY US: Guilford Press.

Resick, P. A., & Schnicke, M. K. (1993). *Cognitive processing therapy for rape victims: A treatment manual.* Thousand Oaks, CA US: Sage Publications, Inc.

Roberts, M. (2000). *Shy Boy. The horse who came in from the wild.* New York: Harper Perennial.

Rodriguez, R. (2002). *Brown: The last discovery of America.* New York: Viking.

Rogers, C. R. (1957). The necessary and sufficient conditions of therapeutic personality change. *Journal of Consulting Psychology, 21*(2), 95–103. doi:10.1037/h0045357

—(1961). *One becoming a person.* Boston: Houghton Mifflin.

Rogers, C. H., Floyd, Seltzer, M. M., Greenberg, J., & Hong, J. (2008). Long-term effects of the death of a child on parents' adjustment in midlife. *Journal of Family Psychology, 22,* 203–11.

Rotter, J. B., Chance, J. E., & Phares, E. J. (1972). *Applications of social learning theory of personality.* New York: Holt, Rinehart & Winston.

Rucker, A. (2007). *The best seat in the house. How I woke up one Tuesday and was paralyzed for life.* New York: HarperCollins.

Ryan, R. M., & Deci, E. L. (2001). On happiness and human potentials: A review of research on hedonic and eudaimonic well-being. *Annual Review of Psychology, 52,* 141–66.

Sakakibara, M., & Hayano, J. (1996). Effect of slowed respiration on cardiac parasympathetic response to threat. *Psychosomatic Medicine, 58*(1), 32–7.

Salsman, J. M., Segerstrom, S. C., Brechting, E. H., Carlson, C. R., & Andrykowski, M. A. (2009). Posttraumatic growth and PTSD symptomatology among colorectal cancer survivors: a 3-month longitudinal examination of cognitive processing. *Psycho-Oncology, 18,* 30–41.

Schroevers, M. J., Helgeson, V. S., Sandernnan, R., & Ranchor, A. V. (2010). Type of social support matters for prediction of posttraumatic growth among cancer survivors. *Psycho-Oncology, 19*(1), 46–53. doi:10.1002/pon.1501

Schuettler, D., & Bols, A. (2011). The path to posttraumatic growth versus posttraumatic stress disorder: Contributions of event centrality and coping. *Journal of Loss and Trauma, 16,* 180–94.

Schwabe, L., Dickinson, A., & Wolf, O. T. (2011). Stress, habits, and drug additions: A psychoneurological perspective. *Experimental and Clinical Psychopharmacology, 19,* 53–63.

Seligman, M., E., & Csikszentmihalyi, M. (2000). Positive psychology: an introduction. *American Psychologist, 55,* 5–14.

Semple, R. J. (2010). Does mindfulness meditation enhance attention? A randomized controlled trial. *Mindfulness, 1*(2), 121–130. doi:10.1007/s12671-010-0017-2

Shafranske, E. P., & Malony, H. N. (1990). Clinical psychologists' religious and spiritual orientations and their practices of psychotherapy. *Psychotherapy, 27,* 72–8.

Shakespeare-Finch, J., & Enders, T. (2008). Corroborating evidence of posttraumatic growth. *Journal of Traumatic Stress, 21,* 421–4.

Shakespeare-Finch, J., Gow, K., & Smith, S. (2005). Personality, coping and posttraumatic growth in emergency ambulance personnel. *Traumatology, 11,* 325–34.

Shakespeare-Finch, J., & Morris, B. (2010). Posttraumatic growth in Australian populations. In T. Weiss & R. Berger (Eds), *Posttraumatic growth and culturally competent practice* (pp. 157–82). Hoboken, NJ: John Wiley & Sons, Inc.

Shapiro, R. (Ed.) (2005). *EMDR solutions: Pathways to healing.* New York: W. W. Norton & Co.

Shapiro, R. (2010). *The trauma treatment handbook: Protocols across the spectrum.* New York: W. W. Norton & Co.

Sharpless, B. A., & Barber, J. P. (2011). A clinician's guide to PTSD treatments for returning veterans. *Professional Psychology: Research And Practice, 42*(1), 8–15. doi:10.1037/a0022351

Shay, J. (1994). *Achilles in Vietnam: Combat trauma and the undoing of character.* New York: Atheneum.

Shay, J. J. (1996). "Okay, I'm here, but I'm not talking!" Psychotherapy with the reluctant male. *Psychotherapy, 33,* 503–13.

Shear, M., & Mulhare, E. (2008). Complicated grief. *Psychiatric Annals, 38*(10), 662–70. doi:10.3928/00485713-20081001-10

Showers, C. J., & Ryff, C. D. (1996). Self-differentiation and well-being in a life transition. *Personality And Social Psychology Bulletin, 22*(5), 448–460. doi:10.1177/0146167296225003

Silvia, P. J. (2011). Evaluating self-reflection and insight as self-conscious traits. *Personality and Individual Differences, 50,* 234–7.

Solnit, R. (2009). *A paradise built in hell: The extraordinary communities that arise in disaster.* New York : Viking.

Spiegel, D. (2010). Hypnosis in the treatment of posttraumatic stress disorders. In S. Lynn, J. W. Rhue, I. Kirsch, S. Lynn, J. W. Rhue, I. Kirsch (Eds), *Handbook of clinical hypnosis, 2nd Ed.* (pp. 415–32). Washington, DC US: American Psychological Association.

Spitzer, C., Barnow, S., Volzke, H., Ulrich, J., Freyberger, H. J., & Grabe, H. J. (2009). Trauma, posttraumatic stress disorder, and physical illness: findings from the general population. *Psychosomatic Medicine, 71,* 1012–17.

Sprang, G., Clark, J. J., & Whitt-Woosley, A. (2007). Compassion fatigue, compassion satisfaction, and burnout: factors impacting a professional's quality of life. *Journal of Loss and Trauma, 12,* 259–80.

Stapel, D. A., & Lonneke, A. J. D. What drives self-affirmation effects? On the importance of differentiating valued affirmation and attributed affirmation. *Journal of Social and Clinical Psychology, 101,* 34–45.

Stockton, H., Hunt, N., & Joseph, S. (2011). Cognitive processing, rumination, and posttraumatic growth. *Journal of Traumatic Stress, 24,* 85–92.

Stuart, R. B. (2004). Twelve practical suggestions for achieving multicultural competence. *Professional Psychology: Research and Practice, 35,* 3–9.

Taku, K. (2011). Commonly-defined and individually-defined posttraumatic growth in the US and Japan. *Personality and Individual Differences, 51,* 188–93.

Taku, K, Cann, A., Calhoun, L. G., & Tedeschi, R. G. (2008). The factor structure of the Posttraumatic Growth Inventory: A comparison of five models using confirmatory factor analysis. *Journal of Traumatic Stress, 21,* 158–164.

Taylor, S. E. (1989). *Positive Illusions.* New York: Basic Books.

Taylor, S. E., & Brown, J. D. (1988). Illusion and well-being: A social-psychological perspective on mental health. *Psychological Bulletin, 103,* 193–210.

—(1994). Positive illusions and well-being revisited: Separating fact from fiction. *Psychological Bulletin, 116,* 21–7.

Taylor, S. (2003). Outcome Predictors for Three PTSD Treatments: Exposure Therapy, EMDR, and Relaxation Training. *Journal of Cognitive Psychotherapy, 17*(2), 149–61. doi:10.1891/jcop.17.2.149.57432

Tedeschi, R. G., & Calhoun, L. G. (1995). *Trauma and transformation: Growing in the aftermath of suffering.* Thousand Oaks, CA: Sage.

—(1996). The Posttraumatic Growth Inventory: Measuring the positive legacy of trauma. *Journal of Traumatic Stress, 9,* 455–71.

—(2004). *Helping bereaved parents: A clinician's guide.* New York: Brunner-Routledge.

—(2006). Expert companions: Posttraumatic growth in clinical practice. In L. G. Calhoun & R. G. Tedeschi, *Handbook of Posttraumatic growth: Research and practice* (pp. 291–310). Mahwah, NJ: Lawrence Erlbaum Associates.

Triplett, K. N., Tedeschi, R. G., Cann, A., Calhoun, & Reeve, C. L. (2012). Posttraumatic growth, meaning in life, and life satisfaction in response to trauma. *Psychological trauma: Theory, Research, Practice, and Policy, 4,* 400–10.

Vishnevsky, T., Cann, A., Calhoun, L. G., Tedeschi, R. G., & Demakis, G. J. (2010). Gender differences in self-reported posttraumatic growth: A meta-analysis. *Psychology of Women Quarterly, 34,* 110–20.

Wachtel, P. L. (2011). *Therapeutic communication, knowing what to say when (2nd Ed.).* New York: Guilford Press.

Wagner, K. G., & Calhoun, L. G. (1991). Perceptions of social support by suicide survivors and their social networks. *Omega: Journal of Death and Dying, 24,* 61–73.

Walsh, R. (2011). Lifestyle and mental health. *American Psychologist, 66,* 579–92.

Washburn, M. (June 12, 2011). Applauding the airliner on which lives changed. [Web log post]. Retrieved from http://www.charlotteobserver.com/2011/06/11/2371846/applauding-the-airliner-on-which.html

Weiss, T. (2002). Posttraumatic growth in women with breast cancer and their husbands: An intersubjective validation study. *Journal of Psychosocial Oncology, 20,* 65–80.

—(2004). Correlates of posttraumatic growth in married breast cancer survivors. *Journal of Social and Clinical Psychology, 23,* 733–46.

Weiss, T., & Berger, R. (2010). *Posttraumatic growth and culturally competent practice.* Hoboken, NJ: John Wiley & Sons Inc.

Wilcox, S. (2010). Social relationships and PTSD symptomatology in combat veterans. *Psychological trauma: Theory, Research, Practice, and Policy, 2,* 175–82.

Wild, N., & Paivio, S. (2003). Psychological adjustment, coping, and emotion regulation as predictors of posttraumatic growth. *Journal of Aggression, Maltreatment and Trauma, 8,* 97–122.

Wilson, J., Friedman, M., & Lindy, J. (Eds) (2001). *Treating psychological trauma and PTSD.* New York: Guilford Press.

Wolchik, S. A., Coxe, S., Tein, J. Y., Sandler, I. N., & Ayers, T. S. (2009). Six-year longitudinal predictors of posttraumatic growth in parentally bereaved adolescents and young adults. *Omega: Journal of Death and Dying, 58*(2), 107–28. doi:10.2190/OM.58.2.b

Wong, P. T. P. (2012). From logotherapy to meaning-centered counseling and therapy. In P. T. P. Wong (Ed.). *The human quest for meaning, 2nd Ed.* (pp. 619–47). New York: Routledge.

Wrosch, C., Scheier, M. F., Miller, G., & Carver, C. S. (2012). When meaning is threatened: The importance of goal adjustment for psychological and physical health. In P. T. P. Wong (Ed.). *The human quest for meaning, 2nd Ed.* (pp. 539–57). New York: Routledge.

Yadin, E., & Foa, E. B. (2007). Cognitive Behavioral Treatments for Posttraumatic Stress Disorder. In L. J. Kirmayer, R. Lemelson, M. Barad, L. J. Kirmayer, R. Lemelson, & M. Barad (Eds), *Understanding trauma: Integrating biological, clinical, and cultural perspectives* (pp. 178–93). New York: Cambridge University Press.

Yalom, I. (1980). *Existential psychotherapy.* New York: Basic Books.

Yalom, I. D. (2009). *Staring at the sun: overcoming the terror of death.* San Francisco: Jossey-Bass.

Younoszai, B. (1993). Mexican American perspectives related to death. In D. P. Irish, K. F. Lundquiat, & V. J. Nelsen (Eds.), Ethnic variations in dying, death, and grief: Diversity in universality (pp. 67–78). Washington, DC: Taylor & Francis.

Yuen, A. C., & Sander, J. W. (2010). Can slow breathing exercises improve seizure control in people with refractory epilepsy? A hypothesis. *Epilepsy and Behavior, 18*(4), 331–4. doi:10.1016/j.yebeh.2010.05.019

Yuval, N., DiGrande, L., & Adams, B. G. (2011). Posttraumatic stress disorder following the September 11, 2001 terrorist attacks: A review of the literature among highly exposed populations. *American Psychologist, 66,* 429–46.

Zoellner, T., & Maercker, A. (2006). Posttraumatic growth and psychotherapy, in L. G. Calhoun & R. G. Tedeschi (Eds), *Handbook of posttraumatic growth: Research and practice* (pp. 334–54). Mahwah, NJ: Lawrence Erlbaum Associates.

Index of Authors

Index of Subjects